5.20

THE NEW WEBSTER'S GRAMMAR GUIDE

Prepared By

Madeline Semmelmeyer, M.A.
and
Donald O. Bolander, M.A., Litt. D.

A Complete Handbook on English Grammar,
Correct Usage and Punctuation

This handbook is an abridgement of
Practical English.

This handbook is an abridgement of
Practical English, copyright 1968, 1965,
1955 by Career Institute, Inc.

This Berkley book contains the complete
text of the original hardcover edition.

THE NEW WEBSTER'S GRAMMAR GUIDE

A Berkley Book / published by arrangement with
Lexicon Publications, Inc.

PRINTING HISTORY
Lexicon edition published 1987
Berkley edition / February 1991

ISBN: 0-425-12557-2

A BERKLEY BOOK ® TM 757,375
Berkley Books are published by The Berkley Publishing Group,
200 Madison Avenue, New York, New York 10016.
The name "BERKLEY" and the "B" logo
are trademarks belonging to Berkley Publishing Corporation.

PRINTED IN THE UNITED STATES OF AMERICA

10 9 8 7 6 5 4

Purpose of This Book

The purpose of this *Handbook* is to provide a quick, easy-to-use guide to grammar, correct usage, and punctuation. It is intended for use in the business office, in the home, and in school. Secretaries, writers, teachers, and students, will find it especially useful.

The *Handbook* is divided into 25 sections or chapters each covering an important aspect or problem in English. The book is designed so that it may be used as a step-by-step complete self-study English review. But, in addition, it is a complete reference handbook for day-to-day use whenever a question arises concerning English usage or punctuation.

Special Features

Complete Table of Contents

Starting on page iv, is a detailed table of contents for use in finding subtopics within each chapter.

Clear Explanations and Examples

Throughout the book, each explanation is followed by one or more specific examples. The examples clarify the principles and rules of good English usage.

TABLE OF CONTENTS

I. THE PARTS OF SPEECH—I

When we speak and write, we use words to express our thoughts and ideas. The English language has thousands of words, but all of them fall into eight groups or classes known as the *parts of speech*. The following names have been given to the *parts of speech:*

Nouns   Pronouns   Verbs

Adjectives   Adverbs   Prepositions

Conjunctions   Interjections

Each group has its special work to do. *Nouns* are the names of persons, places, and things. *Pronouns* take the place of nouns. *Adjectives* and *adverbs* help express the ideas that give color and more definite meanings to nouns, verbs, and other words. *Conjunctions* are joining or connecting words.

Words, then, are the tools of communication. Like any other tool, a word may be used for different purposes at different times. For example, a word might be used as a noun in one sentence and as a verb in another sentence. Another word might be used as a preposition in one sentence and as an adverb in another sentence. All words do not have more than one use, but many words do.

The most important fact concerning any word is its *function* or use in a particular sentence. If you keep this fact in mind, you will have no difficulty in understanding the simple principles that govern the relationship of words in sentences.

NOUNS
WORDS USED AS NAMES

A **noun** is one of the most important words that you use when either speaking or writing. It is the word that tells what you are talking about. *A noun is a word that names something.* There are names for *persons*, *animals*, *places*, and *objects* that

1

can be pointed out and recognized. There are also names for *substances*, *qualities*, *actions*, and *measures* of time or quantity. The following list includes examples of different kinds of nouns.

Persons:	soldier—Jane—friend
Animals:	elephant—mouse—zebra
Places:	home—Chicago—camp
Objects:	desk—picture—computer
Substances:	iron—air—water—food
Qualities:	kindness—heroism—beauty
Actions:	climbing—cooking—reading
Measures:	year—pound—inch—day

Nouns Used in Sentences

The words in *italics* in the following sentences are nouns.

The *soldier* is wearing his new *uniform*.

Chicago is a great industrial *city*.

Iron is a useful *metal*.

PRONOUNS
SUBSTITUTES FOR NOUNS

You will often find it necessary to refer to a *name* a number of times in a single sentence. This repetition usually results in a sentence that is very awkward or monotonous. You can readily see what might happen from the following illustration:

Jack went to *Jack's* closet and took out *Jack's* new suit because *Jack* was going to a dance given by *Jack's* company.

In this sentence the word *Jack* is stated five times. This awkward repetition of the word *Jack* and *Jack's* could be avoided by substituting another part of speech for these words.

Jack went to *his* closet and took out *his* new suit because *he* was going to a dance given by *his* company.

2

The words *his* and *he* used in the revision of the sentence are called **pronouns.** They are substitutes for the noun *Jack.* The prefix **pro** in the word pronoun means *for.* The word **pronoun** simply means *for a noun, or in place of a noun.*

In the following sentences, the pronouns and the nouns to which they refer are underlined.

<u>Mary</u> said <u>she</u> was going.
The <u>men</u> forgot <u>their</u> tickets.
The <u>officer</u> blew <u>his</u> whistle.

Commonly Used Pronouns

You should be familiar with the pronouns in common use. For that reason a list of pronouns is a handy reference guide. Whenever you are not certain whether a word is a pronoun, refer to the following list. In a short time you will be familiar with most of them.

I	she	this	several
my	her	that	other
mine	hers	these	another
me	it	those	anybody
we	its	all	everybody
our	they	any	nobody
ours	their	both	somebody
us	theirs	each	no one
you	them	either	someone
yours	which	neither	everyone
your	what	few	one
he	who	many	whoever
his	whose	none	whosoever
him	whom	some	anyone

VERBS
ACTION AND LINKING VERBS

The **verb** is the most important part of speech. *It is the only*

3

part of speech that can make a statement about the subject.
The subject is the part of a sentence that names the person, place, or thing that is talked about. If you wanted to write or say something about a *hunter*, you could not complete your statement without the use of a verb. You must have a verb in every sentence. The following illustration will make this clear.

The hunter *shot* the deer.
(The verb is the word *shot*.)

If you take the verb *shot* out of the sentence, you have left the words, *the hunter, the deer,* but you do not have a complete thought. You need a verb to state what the hunter did to the deer. When you supply a verb, you have a complete statement.

Most of the verbs in common use express **action.** The action is not always physical action like the action expressed in the sentence, *The hunter shot the deer*. In the sentence, *I solved the problem,* the meaning of the verb *solved* implies both mental and physical activity.

In the sentence, *The engineer built a bridge,* all the types of activity that went on until the bridge was completed are implied in the verb *built*. The same would be true of the verb *made* in the sentence, *The chef made a cake*. All the verbs in the following sentences express action of some kind:

The painter *decorated* the hall.
I *pricked* my finger.
The manager *wrote* a letter.
The president *called* a meeting.

A small, but very important group of verbs, *do not* express action. The verb **to be** is the most important verb in this group. The most common forms of the verb *to be* include *is, are, was* and *were*. Since the verb *to be* does not express action, It must have another function in the sentence. With the help of some other word or words, it makes a statement about the *condition*

4

of the subject, or the person, place, or thing that is talked about.

In the sentence, *Henry is ill,* the verb *is* does not express action of any kind, but it serves two purposes in the sentence. With the help of the word *ill* it makes a statement about the subject, *Henry.* It also serves to connect the word *ill* with *Henry.* The sentence really means *ill Henry,* but you need the verb *is* to make the statement a complete sentence. Because the verb has this connecting function, it is called a **linking verb.**

From the following illustrations, you will see that the verb *to be* with the help of some other word describes or explains the condition of the subject in some way. The verb *is* is a form of the verb *to be.*

My uncle *is* a famous surgeon.
   (classifies uncle as surgeon)
Mother *is* very happy.
   (describes the condition of mother)
Her dress *is* beautiful.
   (describes dress)

VERB PHRASES
PRINCIPAL AND AUXILIARY VERBS

A *verb* is not always a single word. *When the verb is composed of two or more words, it is called a* **verb phrase.** The verb form at the end of the verb phrase is always the *principal verb.* It is the verb form that indicates the nature of the action, if the verb expresses action. The other verb forms in the verb phrase are called *auxiliary verbs* or *helping verbs.*

The men *work* in the fields.
The men *are working* in the fields.
The men *have been working.*
The men *must have been working.*

In the first sentence the verb consists of one word, the verb *work*. The verb *work* tells the kind of action that is going on. The verb in the second sentence consists of two words. The principal verb is *working*. The auxiliary, or helping verb is *are*. The verb phrase is *are working*. The verb phrase in the third sentence is *have been working*. The principal verb is *working*, and the two helping verbs are *have been*. The verb phrase in the fourth sentence is *must have been working*. The principal verb is *working* and the three helping verbs are *must have been*.

One of the first things you should learn to do in your study of grammar is to be able to identify the verb or the verb phrase in any sentence. Some persons have trouble in deciding what words belong in the verb phrase. You will never encounter this difficulty if you become familiar with the commonly used auxiliary verbs. A list of these auxiliary verbs follows. You should refer to this list constantly until you become familiar with the verbs that help make verb phrases.

Commonly Used Auxiliary Verbs

am	have been	could
is	had been	would
are	has been	should
was	shall	must
were	will	should have
will be	do	would have
shall be	did	must have
could be	does	should have been
have	may	could have been
has	can	must have been
had	might	

Verb Phrases Used in Sentences

In the following sentences, the words in *italics* are verb phrases.

You *will receive* the money.
He *was talking* with the manager.
The building *was destroyed* by fire.

2. THE PARTS OF SPEECH—II

Chapter One explained how *nouns, pronouns, verbs,* and *verb phrases* function in English. With these three parts of speech you can build the framework of any sentence. But it is only a framework. The sentence that contains only a noun or a pronoun and a verb is not a very interesting sentence. It does not give very specific information, or present a very interesting picture. Such sentences become very monotonous if repeated often, as you will readily see from the following illustrations:

Birds fly.	Dogs bark.
Men work.	She knits.
He swims.	They sing.

ADJECTIVES-Modifiers

You will generally find it necessary to add other parts of speech to a skeleton sentence to make the meaning clearer and more exact. You can add words to nouns and pronouns that tell *what kind, what color, which one,* etc. If you wanted to tell about the hat a woman was wearing, you would describe the hat in some way. You might say that it was a *large* hat, an *atrocious* hat, or a *red* hat, depending upon the meaning which you intended to convey.

When you add one or more of these *describing words* to hat, you give a clearer picture of what the hat is like. *Words which add new ideas to nouns and pronouns are called* **adjectives.**

The adjective not only describes by telling what kind or what color, but it may limit the meaning by telling *which* hat, *whose* hat, or the *number* of hats. For example, you might limit the meaning by saying *that* hat, *Fred's* hat, *two* hats, or *several* hats.

In grammar, we say that the adjective *modifies* the meaning of the noun or pronoun. The word **modify** means *to change the meaning slightly* by *describing* or *limiting* the meaning to a certain kind or to a certain number.

When we speak of a hat as an *attractive* hat, we are limiting the meaning because we are leaving out all the hats that are not attractive. If a word describes, limits, or restricts the meaning in any way, it is called a **modifier.** This is an important term that is frequently used in grammar.

The words *a, an,* and *the* are adjectives although in grammar they are called **articles.** The word *the* is called the *definite* article. The words *a* and *an* are called the *indefinite articles.* When we say, *the* book on *the* table, we are pointing out a particular book on a particular table. When we say, *I have a book,* no specific or particular book is indicated.

Adjectives Modifying Nouns

The following examples show how adjectives modify nouns and how their use makes the meaning clearer or more explicit.

long road	*good* friend	*rainy* day
rusty nail	*worthy* cause	*rapid* typist
old piano	*steep* hill	*essential* parts

ADVERBS-Modifiers

Another interesting group of words that serve as modifiers are **adverbs.** The prefix *ad* in the word adverb means *to, toward,* or *in addition to.* An adverb is a word that you *add to a verb to modify or expand the meaning of the verb.* Adverbs may also modify adjectives or other adverbs. In this unit we shall consider the adverb as a modifier of the verb. A later unit will give you the other uses of an adverb.

Adverbs are easy to identify because they usually answer the questions *when, where, how, in what manner,* or *to what extent* or *degree*. The following illustrations will make this clear:

You must set up the copy *now*.
 (*Now* tells when to set it up.)
We put the desk *there*.
 (*There* tells where it was put.)
Mary walks *gracefully*.
 (*Gracefully* tells how she walks.)

When we say, *The paper is issued weekly,* the adverb *weekly* introduces an additional idea of *time*. The adverb *weekly* makes the meaning explicit because we know *how often* or *when* the paper is issued. When we say, *Dandelions grow everywhere,* we have introduced the idea of *place*, or we tell *where* the dandelions grow. In the sentence, *We walked farther into the forest,* we have added the idea of *extent* or the *degree to which*. The adverbs in the preceding sentences are called adverbs of *time, place, manner,* or *degree.*

POSITION OF THE ADVERB

Although an adverb often modifies the verb in the sentence, it is not always placed directly after the verb. Sometimes the adverb introduces the sentence. In this position it gives more emphasis. At times the adverb is placed between the parts of the verb phrase. Study the following sentences carefully. Note the position of the adverb.

Sometimes I take a walk in the woods.
Jack *usually* leaves the house at seven.
We added a room to our house *recently*.
I have *always* admired him.

PREPOSITIONS
Words That Show a Relationship

Another important part of speech is the **preposition**. A preposition is not a modifier. The only parts of speech that are modifiers are adjectives and adverbs. The preposition has a different function to perform in the sentence. *A preposition shows the relationship that exists between certain words in a sentence.*

The word *preposition* comes from two Latin words which mean *placed before*. A preposition is a word that is *placed before some noun or pronoun*. It shows the relationship that exists between that noun or pronoun and some other word in the sentence. When we say "a bag *for* the mail," the word *for* is a preposition. It shows a relationship between *bag* and *mail*. The word *mail* which follows the preposition is called the **object** of the *preposition*.

In the sentence, *The accident occurred on the bridge*, the word *on* is a preposition. The preposition *on* is followed by the word *bridge* which is called its object. The entire group of words, *on the bridge*, is called a **prepositional phrase.** The preposition *on* shows the relation between the noun *bridge* and the verb *occurred*. The entire phrase *on the bridge* tells where the accident occurred.

We might use a number of prepositions to show the relationship between the noun *bridge* and the verb *occurred*. Each preposition would show a slightly different type of relationship, as you will readily see from the following illustrations:

The accident occurred *under* the bridge.
The accident occurred *near* the bridge.
The accident occurred *above* the bridge.
The accident occurred *behind* the bridge.
The accident occurred *beneath* the bridge.

CONJUNCTIONS-Connecting Words

In many sentences you need words that serve to join words or groups of words. In grammar, words that have this connecting function are called **conjunctions.**

The word *conjunction* comes from two Latin words which mean to *join with* or to *join together*. In the sentence, *Jane and Alice are secretaries*, the word *and* connects the two nouns,

11

Jane and *Alice*. The word *and* in this sentence is a conjunction. In the sentence, *The manager or his secretary will see you,* the word *or* connects the words *manager* and *secretary*. The word *or* in this sentence is a conjunction. In the sentence, *Her small but attractive apartment is for rent,* the word *but* joins the words *small* and *attractive*.

The conjunctions that were used in the preceding illustrations were *and*, *but*, and *or*. These conjunctions always connect words or groups of words of equal rank. For the present, we shall limit our discussion to the use of these three conjunctions. In the following sentences, the underlined words are the words joined by the conjunction.

Mark drives too fast *and* too recklessly.
  (joins two adverbs)
He *or* I will audit the account.
  (joins two pronouns)
I fell *and* broke my arm.
  (joins two verbs)
It is a large *but* attractive home.
  (joins two adjectives)

INTERJECTIONS-Exclamatory Words

In English we have a number of words that are used to express strong feeling or sudden emotion. Words that serve this purpose are called **interjections.** The word *interjection* comes from two Latin words which mean *to throw between*. Interjections are really thrown into the sentence to express some type of emotion such as disgust, joy, excitement, enthusiasm, etc.

Interjections have no grammatical relation to any word or group of words in the sentence. In grammar we call words of this type *independent elements*. Sometimes words which are independent elements stand for an entire sentence. The following illustrations show the kinds of words that are commonly

12

used as interjections. The interjections are in *italics*.

Alas! This is the end!
Hey! Where are you going?
Bah! I can't believe that.
Pshaw! Why did I do that?

The words classified as interjections in the preceding illustrations *are always interjections*. In addition to such words, nouns, pronouns, adjectives, and other parts of speech *are often used* as interjections.

Heavens! I cut my finger.
Good! I'm glad to hear that.
Horrors! Look at that hat!
Well! When are you going?

FUNCTION OF WORDS

One of the most important things to learn about the English language is the fact that *the same words are often used as different parts of speech*. A word may perform a certain function in one sentence and an entirely different function in another sentence.

Adjectives are commonly used as nouns, and nouns are frequently used as adjectives. The same word may function both as an adverb and as a preposition. Almost any type of word may be used as an interjection. The following sentences show how words function as different parts of speech:

The *light* in my study is poor.
   (*Light* is a noun.)
Please *light* the candles.
   (*Light* is a verb.)
Her hat is a *light* shade of blue.
   (*Light* is an adjective.)

Father is a *fast* driver.
　(*Fast* is an adjective.)
Father drives too *fast*.
　(*Fast* is an adverb.)
I *fast* one day every week.
　(*Fast* is a verb.)

You should become acquainted with the words that are commonly used as prepositions. A list of these prepositions is given here for your reference. Refer to this list repeatedly until you are able to identify the prepositions that are in common use.

A List of Commonly Used Prepositions

above	behind	for	since
about	below	from	to
across	beneath	in	toward
after	beside	inside	through
against	between	into	under
along	beyond	like	until
among	by	near	up
around	down	of	upon
at	during	off	with
before	except	on	within

3. THE SENTENCE

When a number of words (parts of speech) are put together in such a way that they express a **complete thought,** you have a *sentence*. The sentence may consist of one word, or it may consist of as many as three hundred words. The tendency in modern writing is to use short, effective sentences. Twenty words is about the average length in present-day writing.

Often those who are beginning the study of language find it difficult to understand what is meant by a *complete thought*. Some students punctuate parts of sentences as if they were sentences because they do not realize that some essential element is missing. None of the following groups of words are sentences, although they are punctuated as if they were complete.

The officers of our company.
Enjoyed the banquet.
On the top of the hill.

These groups of words are not sentences because they lack something that is necessary in order to express a complete thought. When you examine the first group of words, you will readily see that you know what the writer is talking about. However, the writer did not complete the sentence by telling you what the officers did. The second group of words tells you that somebody enjoyed a banquet. But the author neglected to tell you who it was. The third group of words tells you very little. You have no way of knowing what the writer is talking about.

SUBJECT AND PREDICATE

In order to express a complete thought, a sentence must have both a *subject* and a *predicate*. These are two important grammatical terms used to describe the essential elements of a sentence.

15

The **subject** is the word or group of words that tells us *what or whom the speaker or writer is talking about*. The **predicate** is the part of the sentence *that makes a statement about the subject*. The *predicate* usually tells what the subject is doing, or what is happening to the subject.

Study the following sentences carefully. Note that the subjects have been separated from the predicates so that you will be able to see the relationship between the two parts more easily.

Subject	Predicates
My friend	lives in New York.
The letter	contains exciting news.
Both men	are experienced salesmen.

In the first sentence, I am talking about *my friend*. Therefore, *my friend* is the subject of the sentence. I complete the sentence by making a statement about my friend. I say that my friend *lives in New York*. The predicate is *lives in New York*. This group of words, *My friend lives in New York,* is a sentence because it expresses a complete thought. It has both a subject and a predicate. The other two sentences also have a subject and predicate.

COMPLETE SUBJECT AND COMPLETE PREDICATE

In many sentences the subject or the predicate is only a single word. But more often, the subject consists of two or more words. In grammar, we call the entire subject, regardless of the number of words, the **complete subject.** We call the entire predicate the **complete predicate.**

If the subject of a sentence is a single word, that word is the *complete subject*. If the predicate of the sentence is a single word, that word is the *complete predicate*. In the sentence, *Birds fly*, the word *birds* is the complete subject, and the word *fly* is the complete predicate.

16

SIMPLE SUBJECT AND
SIMPLE PREDICATE

After you have learned how to identify the complete subject and the complete predicate, you can easily find the **simple subject** and the **simple predicate.**

Somewhere in the complete subject you will find the *particular word* about which something is said. That word is the *simple subject*. It is usually either a noun or a pronoun.

Somewhere in the predicate you will find a word that serves as the *key* to the predicate. That word is the *verb,* the most important word in any sentence. If the verb consists of more than one word, it is called a *verb phrase.* In the following examples the simple subjects and predicates are underlined:

The ambassador attended a conference.
The hero of the story had many adventures.
My friend in Boston bought a new car.

Sometimes you will find only one word in the subject or one word in the predicate. In that case, the single word in the subject is the simple subject. It is also the complete subject. The single word in the predicate is the simple predicate and also the complete predicate.

Pronouns are often used as the simple subject and the complete subject. In the sentence, *We are buying a new home*, the pronoun *we* is the simple subject. It is also the complete subject since there are no other words in the subject.

In the sentence, *The building collapsed*, the verb *collapsed* is the simple predicate. It is also the complete predicate since it is the only word in the predicate.

In the following illustrations, the simple subjects and simple predicates are underlined.

Fast driving is often dangerous.
The detectives on the case found the jewels.
Children play.

17

COMPOUND SUBJECT AND
COMPOUND PREDICATE

A sentence may have two or more simple subjects and two or more simple predicates. In the sentence, *Harry and Fred joined a lodge*, there are two simple subjects, *Harry* and *Fred*. The connecting word is *and*. In grammar we say that the sentence has a **compound subject.**

In the sentence, *The stenographer wrote the letter and mailed it*, there are two predicate verbs, *wrote* and *mailed*. The connecting word is *and*. This sentence has a **compound predicate.**

Some sentences have a compound subject and a compound predicate. In the sentence, *Alice and Jane washed the curtains and ironed them*, there are two simple subjects and two simple predicates. The subject nouns are *Alice* and *Jane*. The two predicate verbs are *washed* and *ironed*. In both cases, the connecting word is *and*.

The following sentences contain either a compound subject, a compound predicate, or both.

Corn and beans are grown in the valley.
(*compound subject*)
I attended the lecture and took notes.
(*compound predicate*)
The boys and girls sang and danced at the club.
(*compound subject and compound predicate*)

SENTENCE FRAGMENTS

If you have studied this unit carefully, you will have a thorough understanding of the essential elements of a sentence. But even persons who have this knowledge often punctuate groups of words as sentences when one or both of the essential elements are missing.

Any incomplete group of words punctuated as if it were a sentence is called a *sentence fragment* or a *fragmentary sentence*. As you know, a fragment is only a piece or a part of the whole. A fragment always refers to something that is incomplete.

A fragmentary sentence always lacks one or both of the essential elements of a sentence. That is, either the subject or the predicate, or both the subject and predicate are missing. Whenever you are in doubt about a particular sentence, apply this test: Does the group of words contain both a subject and a predicate? Does it express a complete thought?

Very often the subject of the sentence is missing. The following group of words is *not* a sentence because it does not tell who it is that the writer is talking about:

Interviewed the candidate.

(This is not a sentence.)

The president interviewed the candidate.

(This is a complete sentence.)

The sentence was completed by supplying a subject, *The president*.

Sometimes the predicate is missing. The following group of words is *not* a sentence because the entire predicate is missing:

The sound of footsteps.

(This is not a sentence.)

The sound of footsteps *alarmed us*.

(This is a complete sentence.)

The use of fragmentary or incomplete sentences is an unsatisfactory way of communicating your ideas. Surprising as it may seem, sentence fragments similar to the following examples can be found repeatedly in letters sent out by reputable business firms. Check the letters of your company. You may be amazed at what you find. Be sure you do not use fragments

19

in your own personal writing.

Received your letter this morning.
Will send order at once.
Have shipped your order.
Hoping this meets with your approval.

4. SENTENCE PATTERNS

In Chapter Three it was explained that a sentence must express a complete thought. It must also have both a subject and a predicate. This unit shows how it is possible to express a complete thought in a variety of ways. You should become familiar with the different ways of arranging words in sentences and the different sentence patterns that are the result of these arrangements.

KINDS OF SENTENCES

Sentences fall into four groups according to the purpose the sentence serves and the manner in which the thought is expressed. Some sentences simply *make statements*. Some sentences *ask questions*. Another type of sentence *gives a command* or *makes a request*. The last group is the kind of sentence that *expresses strong feeling* or *sudden emotion*.

In grammar, the sentence that makes a statement is called a **declarative sentence.** The sentence that asks a question is called an **interrogative sentence.** The sentence that gives a command or makes a request is called an **imperative sentence,** and the sentence that expresses strong feeling is called an **exclamatory sentence.** Following are examples of the four types of sentences:

My friend is a business executive.
    (*declarative sentence*)

Have you entered the contest?
    (*interrogative sentence*)

Clear the road at once!
    (*imperative sentence*—command)

Please shut the door.
    (*imperative sentence*—request)

What a tragedy this is!

(*exclamatory sentence*)

If you examine the preceding illustrations carefully, you will notice that the *declarative sentence* ends with a *period*. The *interrogative sentence ends with a question mark* (?). Sometimes the *imperative sentence* ends with an *exclamation mark* (!) and sometimes it ends with a *period*. If the command is given in a very emphatic or decisive manner, an exclamation mark is placed at the end. A mild request always ends with a period. An *exclamatory sentence* usually ends with an *exclamation mark*. Briefly summarized, then:

A **declarative** sentence *makes a statement*.

An **interrogative** sentence *asks a question*.

An **imperative** sentence gives a *command* or makes a *request*.

An **exclamatory** sentence expresses *strong feeling* or *sudden emotion*.

INVERTED ORDER

You have probably observed that the four types of sentences follow certain patterns of word arrangement. These patterns will now be discussed in more detail.

Every sentence has a basic structure or framework. This is true of all four types of sentences—*declarative, interrogative, imperative,* and *exclamatory.* This framework, as you already know, consists of the subject noun or pronoun and the predicate verb.

There are a number of ways of introducing the subject in a declarative sentence. The **normal order,** or the grammatical order, is *subject first,* followed by the predicate. If you always followed this pattern, your sentences would soon become monotonous and uninteresting. The following illustration will make this clear. The sentences in this paragraph sound very much like the sentences in a primer or in a first reader.

I like this book. It is a book about Mexico. My friend sent this book to me. My friend lives in New York. She speaks Spanish.

In this short paragraph, all the sentences follow the same pattern—subject first, followed by the predicate. You can give more variety to your sentence patterns by placing words in unusual positions.

You can put the subject after the verb or place it at the very end of the sentence. Varying the position of the subject gives you an opportunity to place other words at the beginning of the sentence to give them more emphasis. This also makes our sentences more interesting.

On my desk I found an interesting book about Mexico.

In this sentence, the subject is placed after the group of words, or the phrase, *on my desk*. This arrangement throws the phrase to the front of the sentence and gives it more emphasis.

When the subject of the sentence does not appear in its normal position, we say that the order of the sentence is inverted, or turned around. Always remember that *normal* or grammatical order *means subject first,* followed by the predicate. Examine the following sentences carefully. Note the position of the subject in the two sentences.

The *band* marched down the street.
Down the street marched the *band*.

The first sentence is in normal, or grammatical order. The subject noun *band* appears at the beginning of the sentence. The verb *marched* follows the subject.

The second sentence is the same sentence in **inverted order.** The subject noun *band* now appears at the end of the sentence. The verb *marched* comes before the subject. A phrase, *Down the street*, appears at the beginning of the sentence.

An adverb often introduces a sentence. The following sentence begins with an adverb, and not with the subject.

Suddenly the train stopped. (*inverted order*)
The train stopped *suddenly*. (*normal order*)

Some persons find it difficult to determine the true subject when a sentence is not in grammatical order. This difficulty can be avoided by *transposing* the sentence and putting it back in normal order. The only purpose in transposing a sentence is to see the grammatical relations more clearly.

Sometimes when you put a sentence back in grammatical order by transposing it, you will find that the transposed sentence is not so smooth as the original sentence. However, the following sentence is just as effective in either order.

Along the road we passed a number of army trucks.
We passed a number of army trucks *along the road*.

Whenever you are dealing with a sentence in inverted order, you should transpose it before you attempt to analyze the sentence from the grammatical point of view.

INTERROGATIVE SENTENCE PATTERNS

In asking a question, you seldon start with the subject first, as you do in a declarative sentence. For that reason, *the interrogative sentence is generally in inverted order*. Sometimes the interrogative sentence starts with the *verb*. Often it begins with an *adverb,* which is used to ask the question.

Did you bring your camera?
    (introduced by the *verb*)
Where did you buy your watch?
    (introduced by an *adverb*)

In order to see the grammatical constructions in an interrogative sentence that is inverted, you must transpose the sentence and put it in normal order. Sometimes the interrogative sentence becomes a statement when it is transposed.

<u>You</u> <u>did bring</u> your camera.
<u>You</u> <u>did buy</u> your watch where?

IMPERATIVE AND EXCLAMATORY SENTENCE PATTERNS

The imperative sentence presents a different problem. The *subject* of the sentence that gives a command or makes a request *is seldom expressed*. If the subject is not expressed, it is the word *you* understood.

Sound the alarm at once!
    (Subject is not expressed.)
(You) Sound the alarm at once!
    (Subject *you* is understood.)
Please read the announcement.
    (Subject is not expressed.)
(You) Please read the announcement.
    (Subject *you* is understood.)

Sometimes an imperative sentence begins with a noun that indicates the name of the person to whom the command or the request is given. An interrogative sentence may also begin in this way. The point to keep in mind is that such a noun *is not the subject* of the sentence. In fact, it has no grammatical connection with the rest of the sentence. It is an independent element. For that reason, it is separated from the rest of the sentence by a comma. Study the following illustrations carefully:

Imperative Sentence

Fred, please close the door.
    (*Fred* is the person addressed.)
Fred, (you) please close the door.

(Subject is *you* understood.)

Interrogative Sentence

Alice, did you lock the door?
 (*Alice* is a noun in direct address.)
Alice, you did lock the door?
 (Subject is *you* expressed.)

In the first sentence, the word *Fred* is a noun in **direct address** because it names the person spoken to directly. It is not the subject of the sentence. The subject of an imperative sentence is *you* understood. The word *Fred* is set off from the rest of the sentence by a comma to show that it is used *independently*.

In the second sentence, the word *Alice* is a noun in direct address because it names the person spoken to directly. Since this is an interrogative sentence, the subject is expressed. When the sentence is placed in normal order, you can easily see that the subject is *you,* and not Alice.

A noun in *direct address* may appear at the beginning or at the end of the sentence. It may even appear within the sentence.

Fred, please close the door.
 (beginning of the sentence)
Please close the door, *Fred.*
 (end of the sentence)
Come here, *Fred,* and look at this book.
 (within the sentence)

The exclamatory sentence is often expressed in inverted order. In the sentence, *What a feast she spread!,* the subject and the verb appear at the end of the sentence. When the sentence is transposed, the subject appears at the beginning of the sentence and is followed by the verb.

What a feast she spread! (*inverted order*)
She spread what a feast! (*normal order*)

26

How beautiful the sunset is tonight! (*inverted order*)
The sunset is how beautiful tonight! (*normal order*)

What a tragedy that would be! (*inverted order*)
That would be what a tragedy! (*normal order*)

SENTENCES THAT BEGIN WITH "THERE"

Another sentence pattern that we use frequently is the sentence that begins with the word *there*. We have a very good reason for beginning some of our sentences in this way.

When the word *there* is used to introduce the sentence, it is possible to place the subject after the verb. In many cases this results in a much smoother sentence, as you will see from the following illustration:

A heavy frost was last night.
There was a heavy frost last night.

Although the first sentence is in grammatical order, it is a very awkward sentence. The second arrangement results in a much smoother style, but it presents a grammatical problem. In dealing with a sentence that begins with *there,* you must always remember that the word *there* is neither the subject of the sentence, nor an adverbial modifier. It is merely an introductory word which has a special function, that of introducing the sentence.

When the word *there* functions in this way, it is called an **expletive.** The word **expletive** comes from the Latin and means "*added merely to fill up.*" This is a very suitable term because it explains exactly what takes place.

The word *there* merely "fills up" the place normally occupied by the subject. It has no other function in the sentence. Like the noun in direct address, it is an independent construction. When the sentence is transposed, and placed in grammatical order, you should enclose the word *there* in parentheses to show that it is used independently.

There are twelve candidates for the position.
(There) twelve candidates are for the position.

It is important to transpose the sentence beginning with *there* in order to determine the true subject of the sentence. It is also important to determine whether the word *there* is used as an introductory word or whether it is used as an adverb.

There they are. (*There* is an adverb of place.)
They are *there*. (*There* is an adverb of place.)

There were ten men in the band. (*there*—expletive)
(*There*) ten men were in the band. (*there*—expletive)

The coach stood *there* watching the game. (*there*—adverb of place)
There is a telephone directory on the table. (*there*—expletive)
We met *there* last year. (*there*—adverb of place)
There will be some objection to the plan. (*there*—expletive)

The word *it* is also used as an expletive in certain sentence patterns. The use of *it* as an expletive will be discussed in later units.

5. NOUNS
KINDS OF NOUNS

Chapter One explained that a noun is a word used as a name. You also learned that some nouns begin with capital letters, and others begin with small letters. The subject of *capitalization* is very important because it is closely concerned with the division of nouns into groups or classes.

In English, nouns are divided into two main classes called **common nouns** and **proper nouns.** A *common noun* names any one of a class of persons, places, or things. We have a name for all the chairs in the world when we use the common noun *chair*. We have a name for all the lakes in the world when we use the common noun *lake*.

But when we want to name a particular lake, we must give it a special name. The name of a particular lake might be *Lake Louise, Lake George,* or *Lake Michigan.* These particular names are called proper nouns. *A proper noun always begins with a capital letter.*

We have particular names for persons, such as *John Adams, General Eisenhower, Queen Elizabeth,* and *Governor Stevenson.* We also have particular names for certain objects, such as buildings, hotels, theaters, and clubs: *Conway Building, Congress Hotel, Harris Theater,* and *Union League Club.*

Sometimes a common noun names a collection of objects or a group of persons. When we use the word *band* in music, we include under one name all the musicians who play the different instruments. When we use the word *jury,* we include all the members who make up the jury. Nouns that name a group of persons or a collection of objects are called *collective nouns.*

A **common noun** is the name of *any one* of a class of *persons, places,* or *things.*

aviator	ocean	tiger	meat
city	book	lily	desk

A **proper noun** is the name of a *particular person, place,* or *thing*.

Pacific Ocean	Thomas Edison
Chicago	Amazon River
England	Wrigley Building
State Street	Bay of Fundy

A **collective noun** is a common noun whose singular form names a *group* of persons, objects, or acts.

crowd	herd	company	team
army	corps	audience	faculty

Some nouns are *common nouns* in one sentence and *proper nouns* in another sentence.

Common Nouns
Roy is studying to be a doctor.
John's uncle is an engineer.
I went to the theater with May.
We spent the summer at the lake.

Proper Nouns
The family called in Dr. Allen.
Uncle John is a colonel in the army.
The play was given at the Grand Theater.
Did you ever cross Lake Erie?

CAPITALIZATION OF PROPER NOUNS

A student of language should be familiar with the accepted rules regarding the capitalization of *proper nouns* and *proper adjectives*. **Proper adjectives** *are adjectives derived from proper nouns.*

Proper Nouns	**Proper Adjectives**
America	an *American* soldier
Spain	a *Spanish* house
China	a *Chinese* vase

The following list of rules for the capitalization of proper nouns follows accepted, present-day usage:

1. Capitalize names of *particular persons* and *places*.

Mr. Smith   Yankee Stadium
Helen Hayes   Radio City
Senator Clark   Ellis Island

2. Capitalize *geographic names:* continents, countries, states, cities, rivers, mountains, lakes, falls, harbors, valleys, bays, etc.

Africa   Gulf of Mexico
Montana   Rocky Moutains
Pikes Peak   New York Harbor
Cleveland   Long Island

3. Capitalize names of *definite regions, localities,* and *political divisions*.

the Orient   Third Precinct
the Bad Lands   Wheeling Township
the Arctic Circle   French Republic

4. Capitalize names of *bridges, buildings, monuments, parks, ships, automobiles, hotels, forts, dams, railroads, streets,* etc.

Brooklyn Bridge   Michigan Avenue
Fine Arts Building   Plaza Hotel
Statue of Liberty   Eiffel Tower
Central Park   Boulder Dam

5. Capitalize names of *historical events, historical periods,* and *historical documents*.

the Middle Ages   Battle of Gettysburg
World War II   Louisiana Purchase
the Crusades   Fourteenth Amendment
Magna Charta   the Civil War (American)

6. Capitalize names of *governmental bodies* and *departments*.

Bureau of Mines	Civil Service Commission
the Federal Government	Federal Trade Commission
United States Senate	the President's Cabinet
Federal Courts	Supreme Court of the United States

7. Capitalize names of *political parties*, *business* and *fraternal organizations*, *clubs* and *societies*, *companies*, and *institutions*.

Republicans	County Hospital
Democratic Party	John Crerar Library
(or party)	a Shriner
Chapman Chemical	the Elks
Company	Ford Motor Company
Volunteers of America	Rutgers University

8. Capitalize *titles of rank* when they are joined to a person's name.

President Lincoln	Professor Thomas
Senator Lodge	Doctor Hayden
Dr. Allen Reed	Dean Mary Allison
Chancellor Harris	Cardinal Wolsey
Secretary Henderson	His Honor the Mayor

9. Capitalize *days* of the *week*, *months* of the *year*, *holidays*, and *days* of *special observance*, such as feast and fast days.

Monday	Feast of the Passover
September	Mothers's Day
Labor Day	Good Friday
Easter Sunday	Memorial Day

10. You should not capitalize names of the seasons unless they are personified. When something is personified it is represented or considered as if it were a person. Personification is frequently used in poetry.

spring	winter
Spring's warm touch	Winter's icy breath

11. The words *north*, *east*, *south*, and *west* are capitalized when they refer to *sections* of the country. They are not capitalized when they refer to *directions*.

Sections of Countries

the Midwest
the Far West
the Near East

Directions

I travel north on my way home.
The sun rises in the east.
The southern part of Idaho is beautiful.

12. The *special names* given to planets and stars are capitalized. The words *sun*, *moon*, *star*, and *planet* are not capitalized.

Jupiter	The *sun* rose at six that morning.
Venus	The *moon* is a heavenly body.
Mars	A *planet* shines by reflected light.
Milky Way	A *constellation* is a group of stars.

SPECIAL USES OF CAPITAL LETTERS

1. Words derived from proper nouns are usually capitalized. If the word has acquired a special meaning, it is not capitalized.

Capitalized	Not Capitalized
Mongolian race	navy blue
Venetian blinds	china cabinet
Swiss cheese	morocco leather
English tweeds	chinaware
Turkish bath	turkish towel or Turkish towel

2. The principal words in *titles of books, magazines, pictures, songs, articles,* etc., are capitalized. Prepositions, conjunctions, and the articles *a, an,* and *the* are not capitalized unless the title begins with one of these words.

The Last of the Mohicans (book)
The Saturday Evening Post (magazine)
"Outside Our World" (article)
Battle Hymn of the Republic (song)
"Meet the Press" (television prograi)

3. The definite article *the* is not capitalized unless it is the first word of a title. Many titles do not begin with *the.* If the word *the* is within the title, it is written with a small letter. The only way to be sure about the correct form of a title is to check the official form, or the form adopted by the company, publication, etc.

The Christian Science Monitor
The John C. Harris Company
National Geographic Magazine
Pinnacle Oil Company

4. All words referring to the Deity, the Bible, books of the Bible, and other *sacred books* are capitalized.

God, the Father	the Koran
Savior	Genesis
the Trinity	Supreme Being
Talmud	Bible
Book of Job	New Testament

5. The pronoun *I* and the interjection *O* are capitalized. The word *oh* is not capitalized unless it is the first word of a sentence.

"O say! can you see, by the dawn's early light, . . ."
" 'Tis the Star Spangled Banner, oh, long may it wave. . ."

6. Names of school subjects are not capitalized unless they

are names of the languages. Subjects listed in school catalogs as names of special courses are capitalized.

mathematics	History 101
French	Advanced Chemistry II
economics	Economics 345
English	Physics II

7. Capitalize words which show family relationships when they are used with a person's name. The words *father* and *mother* are not capitalized when they are preceded by a pronoun. When used without a pronoun, they are usually capitalized.

Aunt Martha	her cousin
Cousin John	their uncle
Uncle Jack	my father

8. Capitalize the first word in a *compound word that is used as a proper noun*. If the second word in the compound word is a proper noun, it should also be capitalized. Capitalize both parts of *compound titles of distinction*.

Forty-third Street	un-American activities
Army-Navy game	ex-President Eisenhower
The Honorable	Rear Admiral Simpson
John Willis	

9. The names of special departments of business firms may be written with small or with capital letters. In business writing, it is considered good practice to capitalize titles such as *president, secretary, office manager, general superintendent*, etc. They may also be written with small letters.

claim department *or* Claim Department
The Company will reimburse you. (or company)
Our President will see you. (or president)

PLURAL FORMS OF NOUNS

When a noun refers to one person or thing, it is singular in number. When a noun refers to more than one person or thing, it is plural in number. Nouns have special forms to show these distinctions, as you will see from the following illustrations:

Singular	Plural
boy	boys
box	boxes
leaf	leaves
tomato	tomatoes

The plurals of nouns are formed in a number of different ways. Since there are exceptions to almost every one of these methods, you should consult a reliable dictionary whenever you are in doubt regarding a correct plural form. You should also be familiar with the following methods of forming the plurals of nouns:

1. Most nouns add the letter *s* to the singular to form the plural.

lamp	lamps	college	colleges
dance	dances	manager	managers
chief	chiefs	dynamo	dynamos

2. Nouns ending in *s*, *sh*, *ch*, *x*, or *z* form the plural by adding *es*. The plural adds another syllable in the pronunciation.

dress	dresses	couch	couches
match	matches	waltz	waltzes
tax	taxes	loss	losses

3. Nouns ending in *o* preceded by a vowel add *s*. Musical terms ending in *o* add *s*.

Vowel Preceding "o"		Musical Terms	
patio	patios	piano	pianos
rodeo	rodeos	alto	altos

Some nouns ending in *o* preceded by a consonant add *s*. Others add *es*. Some form the plural either way.

Add "s"		Add "es"	
kimono	kimonos	Negro	Negroes
zero	zeros	hero	heroes

Add "s" or "es"

cargo	cargos	cargoes
motto	mottos	mottoes

4. Nouns ending in *y* preceded by a consonant, change the *y* to *i* and add *es*.

party	parties	country	countries
city	cities	enemy	enemies
lady	ladies	berry	berries

5. Nouns ending in *y* preceded by a vowel, usually add *s*. In many cases the vowel before the final *y* is *e*.

alley	alleys	journey	journeys
boy	boys	valley	valleys
key	keys	day	days

6. Some nouns ending in *f* or *fe* change the *f* or the *fe* to *v* and add *es*. Some nouns ending in *f* have two plurals, one in *s* and one in *ves*. Some simply add *s*.

Change to "ves"		Add "s" or Change to "ves"		
wife	wives	scarf	scarfs	scarves
thief	thieves	wharf	wharfs	wharves
half	halves	hoof	hoofs	hooves

7. Some nouns form the plural by a change in the vowel.

man	men	mouse	mice
foot	feet	goose	geese
tooth	teeth	louse	lice

8. Some nouns have the same form for both singular and plural.

Singular and Plural

fish	fish	species	species
sheep	sheep	series	series
Chinese	Chinese	salmon	salmon

9. The plurals of compound nouns are generally formed by adding *s* to the *principal word* in the compound.

mother-in-law	*mothers*-in-law
board of education	*boards* of education
attorney general	*attorneys* general or
	attorney *generals*
court-martial	*courts*-martial

Sometimes *both parts* of the compound are made plural.

| manservant | menservants |
| woman doctor | women doctors |

Sometimes an *s* or *es* is added to the end of the compound. In that case, there is no important word in the compound.

| forget-me-not | forget-me-nots |
| toothbrush | toothbrushes |

Compounds ending in *ful* are made plural by adding *s* to the end of the compound. This rule applies when the same container is filled a number of times.

| spoonful | spoonfuls | handful | handfuls |
| bucketful | bucketfuls | cupful | cupfuls |

10. The plurals of proper names are formed by adding *s* or *es*.

There are three *Ruths* in this class.
The two *Burnses* left the hall.
The *Joneses* and the *Smiths* attended.

The spelling of proper names must not be changed. If we followed the rule for words ending in *y* in the case of *Mary*, we would change the *y* to *i* and add *es*. The name would then be changed to *Marie*, for the plural would be *Maries*. The correct plural of *Mary* is *Marys*.

11. Titles are made plural in several ways. The plural of *Miss* is *Misses;* the plural of *Mr.* is *Messrs. Mrs.* has no plural. The plural of *Madam* is *Mesdames*, which is sometimes used for the plural of *Mrs. Misses* should not be followed by a period. It is not an abbreviation. In the first column of the following examples, the title is made plural. In the second column the name is made plural. Either form is correct.

the *Misses* Thomas   *or*   the Miss *Thomases*
the *Messrs.* Churchill   *or*   the Mr. *Churchills*

Foreign Plurals

Words taken from foreign languages usually retain their foreign plurals. Some of these words are used so commonly that they have acquired an English plural which is formed in the regular way; that is, by adding *s* or *es* to the singular.

The following list gives the foreign and English plurals for some commonly used foreign words. If no English plural is given, the foreign plural is used.

Foreign Word	Foreign Plural	English Plural
alumna (*feminine*)	alumnae	_____
alumnus	alumni	_____

	(*masculine*)	
analysis	analyses	
appendix	appendices	appendixes
bacterium	bacteria	
basis	bases	
cactus	cacti	cactuses
crisis	crises	
criterion	criteria	criterions
curriculum	curricula	curriculums
datum	data	
formula	formulae	formulas
gymnasium	gymnasia	gymnasiums
hypothesis	hypotheses	
index	indices	indexes
madam	mesdames	
medium	media	mediums
memorandum	memoranda	memorandums
parenthesis	parentheses	
phenomenon	phenomena	
radius	radii	radiuses

12. The plural of numbers, letters, signs, and symbols is formed by adding the apostrophe and *s*.

Your *2's* look like your *3's*.
You use too many *ands* in your writing.
  (correct)
or
You use too many *and's* in your writing.
  (correct)
You must always cross your *t's*.
He received three *A's* and two *B's* last semester.

13. The following nouns are used only in the plural. You may find some of them used in the singular, but the general practice is to regard them as plural. When you are in doubt,

consult the dictionary.

trousers	shears	contents
pants	pliers	riches
scissors	scales (weighing)	alms
billiards	nuptials	remains
clothes	gallows	victuals

6. PRONOUNS

In Chapter One you learned that a *pronoun* is a word used in place of a noun. Because pronouns can be used in place of nouns, they avoid the monotonous repetition of nouns. The following illustration shows what happens when we repeat the same noun too often in a sentence:

Alice went to **Alice's** room to dress because **Alice** was going to a reception given by **Alice's** club in **Alice's** honor.

This sentence is very awkward and monotonous because of the tiresome repetition of *Alice* and *Alice's*. When we rewrite the sentence and substitute pronouns for *Alice* and *Alice's*, we have a much better sentence.

Alice went to **her** room to dress because **she** was going to a reception given by **her** club in **her** honor.

You should not only learn how to use pronouns effectively, but you should also learn how to use them correctly. Many of the language errors that are commonly made are errors in the use of pronouns. Mistakes occur because some of the pronouns that we use constantly have a number of different forms.

As a student of English you should know how and when to use the different forms of pronouns. In order to do this, you must be familiar with the changes in form that certain pronouns undergo. To illustrate: The pronoun I is used as the subject of a sentence. When this same pronoun is used as the object of a preposition, the form changes to *me*. It is incorrect to say, "between *you* and I." The correct form to use in this phrase is *me*.

Illustrations of Changes in the Forms of Pronouns

I saw the accident. (The pronoun I is the subject.)
Jane saw **me** at the game. (The pronoun *me* is the object of *saw*.)

42

He *won* the first prize. (The pronoun *he* is the subject).

We met **him** in the lobby. (The pronoun *him* is the object of *met*.)

In the first sentence, the pronoun *I* is used as the **subject** of the sentence. When this same pronoun is used as the **object of a verb,** the form changes to *me*. In the third sentence, the pronoun *he* is the subject of the sentence. When this same pronoun is used as the object of the verb *met*, the form changes to *him*.

KINDS OF PRONOUNS

There are five groups or classes of pronouns in English: **personal** pronouns, **interrogative** pronouns, **demonstrative** pronouns, **indefinite** pronouns, and **relative** pronouns. The personal pronouns include the *compound personal* pronouns, and the relative pronouns include the *compound relative* pronouns.

PERSONAL PRONOUNS

The personal pronouns are the most important group of pronouns. They are also the pronouns that will give you the most trouble unless you are familiar with the various forms that belong to each pronoun.

A **personal pronoun** is a pronoun that shows by its form whether it refers to the *person speaking*, the *person spoken to*, or the *person or thing spoken of*. All the personal pronouns, with the exception of the pronoun *it*, refer to persons. The following sentences show the use of personal pronouns in the first, second, and third person:

I shall spend the winter in Texas. (*I* is the *person speaking*.)

You are working too hard. (*You* is the *person spoken to*.)

He bought a new Ford. (*He* is the *person spoken about*.)

We built the garage. (*We* refers to the *persons speaking*.)

They operate two farms. (*They* refers to the *persons spoken about*.)

Ted has a new radio. **It** is a Zenith. (*It* refers to the *thing spoken about*.)

Jan has two fur coats. **They** are both mink. (*They* refers to the *things spoken about*.)

The pronoun of the **first person** is the pronoun I with its plural form *we*. The pronoun of the **second person** is *you*. The plural form is also *you*. The pronouns of the **third person** are *he, she,* and *it* with the common plural *they* for all three pronouns.

The personal pronouns also have different forms to indicate case. You will learn more about the case of pronouns in Chapter Nine. For the present, you should be familiar with all the forms of the personal pronouns and the pronoun *who* so that you will be able to identify them.

Forms of the Personal Pronouns

1. First person—personal pronouns referring to the *speaker*:

I, my, mine, me (singular)
we, our, ours, us (plural)

2. Second person—personal pronouns referring to the *person spoken to*:

you, your, yours (same forms in both singular and plural)

3. Third person—personal pronouns referring to the *persons* or *things spoken about*:

he, his, him, she, her, hers, it, its (singular)
they, their, theirs, them (plural)

4. Forms of the pronoun **who**:

who, whose, whom

COMPOUND PERSONAL PRONOUNS

Sometimes the word *self* or *selves* is added to certain forms of the personal pronouns. Pronouns formed in this way are called **compound personal pronouns.**

List of Compound Personal Pronouns

myself	herself
yourself	ourselves
himself	yourselves
itself	themselves

Compound personal pronouns are used in two ways: (1) as *reflexive pronouns* and (2) as *intensive pronouns.* A compound personal pronoun is used *reflexively* when the pronoun is the object of the verb. It tells *who* or *what* received *the* action expressed by the verb. In this case the pronoun *always refers back* to the same person or thing as the subject. The following illustration will help to make this clear.

The chef burned himself yesterday.

In this sentence the word *himself* is a compound personal pronoun used as the object of the verb *burned. Himself* refers to the same person as the subject, which is the word *chef.* In other words, *chef* and *himself* are the same person. This is called the **reflexive** use of the compound personal pronoun. It means that the pronoun *refers* or *reflects back* to the subject.

Sometimes the compound personal pronoun is used to give added emphasis to a noun or pronoun in the sentence. This is called the **emphatic** or **intensive** use of the compound personal pronoun.

When a compound personal pronoun is used in this way, it must give emphasis to some noun or pronoun that is already in the sentence. Observe the following sentences carefully. In each sentence you will find that there is a *noun* or a *pronoun* to which the compound personal pronoun refers.

I made the dress <u>myself</u>. (*Myself* intensifies the pronoun I.)

<u>John</u> <u>himself</u> built the canoe. (*Himself* intensifies the noun *John*.)

Incorrect Use of Compound Personal Pronouns

One of the mistakes commonly made in English is to use the compound personal pronoun when there is no word in the sentence to which it refers. These pronouns should never be used as a substitute for a personal pronoun. They should never be used as the subject of the sentence.

My wife and *myself* appreciate your courtesy. (incorrect)

My wife and I appreciate your courtesy. (correct)

The manager and *myself* checked the accounts. (incorrect)

The manager and I checked the accounts. (correct)

He sent the book to John and *myself*. (incorrect)

He sent the book to John and **me.**
(correct)

The first sentence is incorrect because there is no noun or pronoun in the sentence which the pronoun *myself* refers to or gives emphasis to. The second sentence is correct because a *personal pronoun* is used.

Whenever you use a compound personal pronoun in a sentence, always remember that such a pronoun must have an *antecedent,* or a word in the sentence which refers to the same person or thing as the pronoun does. In other words, it must have its own antecedent in the sentence. Do not make mistakes like the following:

Alice and *yourself* were appointed on the committee. (incorrect)

Alice and **you** were appointed on the committee. (correct)

The owner gave Tom and *myself* his old lawn mower. (incorrect)

46

The owner gave Tom and **me** his old lawn mower. (correct)

Everyone in the club has a car as well as *myself*. (incorrect)
Everyone in the club has a car as well as **I**. (correct)

They sent an invitation to the Smiths and *ourselves*. (incorrect)
They sent an invitation to the Smiths and **us**. (correct)

INTERROGATIVE PRONOUNS

Interrogative pronouns are pronouns that are used in asking questions. The interrogative pronouns are *who (whose, whom), which,* and *what.* An interrogative pronoun also has another function to perform in the sentence, just as any other pronoun has. It may be the *subject* of the sentence, or it may be the *object* of the verb or of a preposition.

Who is the director of the band?

For **whom** are you waiting?

What did they say about his speech?

Which is your car?

Whose car did you borrow?

DEMONSTRATIVE PRONOUNS

Demonstrative pronouns are pronouns that point out definite persons, places, or things. There are only two demonstrative pronouns: *this* with its plural *these,* and *that* with its plural *those*.

This is my hat. (A definite hat is pointed out.)
That is your book. (A definite book is pointed out.)
These are the theater tickets. (Definite tickets are pointed out.)
Those are John's shoes. (Definite shoes are pointed out.)

INDEFINITE PRONOUNS

A large group of pronouns are called **indefinite pronouns** because they do not point out particular places, persons, or things.

Somebody took my coat. (*Somebody* is an indefinite pronoun.)

A **few** left the hall early. (*Few* is an indefinite pronoun.)

The following list contains the commonly used indefinite pronouns. Refer to this list, and to the other lists in this unit, whenever you are not sure of the classification of a pronoun.

Commonly Used Indefinite Pronouns

all	everybody	one
any	everyone	one another
anybody	everything	ones
anyone	few	other
anything	many	others
both	neither	several
each	nobody	some
each one	none	somebody
each other	no one	someone
either	nothing	something

RELATIVE PRONOUNS

A **relative pronoun** is a pronoun that joins the clause which it introduces to its own antecedent. The *antecedent* of a pronoun is the noun or pronoun to which it refers. (Clauses will be explained in later chapters.)

The relative pronouns are *who, which, that,* and *what.* The pronoun *who* has two other forms, *whose* and *whom.* When the relative pronoun is combined with *ever* or *soever,* it is called a **compound relative pronoun.**

List of Compound Relative Pronouns

whoever	whosoever	whichsoever
whomever	whatsoever	whomsoever
whatever	whosesoever	whichever

The *relative pronoun* is always found in a clause which it introduces. For that reason, we shall postpone further study of relative pronouns until we take up the study of subordinate clauses.

Use of Relative Pronouns

The following distinctions are generally observed in the use of relative pronouns. A careful writer or speaker always observes these distinctions:

Who is used when the antecedent is a *person*.

That is used to refer to either *persons* or *things*.

Which is used to refer to anything *except persons*.

She is the girl **who** won the award.

(*Who* refers only to persons.)

This is the dog **that** (or **which**) was lost.

(*That* or *which* refers to things.)

She is the girl **that** won the award.

(*That* may refer to persons.)

PRONOUNS USED AS ADJECTIVES

The *possessive forms* of the personal pronouns are often used with nouns in much the same way as adjectives are used to modify nouns. Although they function as adjectives when they are placed before the noun, they still retain the idea of possession. For that reason, they are sometimes called **possessive adjectives** to distinguish them from other types of adjectives.

In the sentence, *Herbert forgot his coat*, the possessive form of the pronoun *he*, which is *his*, is used as an adjective modifying the noun *coat*. It also shows that the coat belongs to Herbert. Therefore, it is called a possessive adjective. All the adjectives in the following sentences show possession. They are called possessive adjectives.

Possessive Forms of Personal Pronouns Used as Adjectives

These are **her** gloves. (modifies *gloves*)

I bought **their** home. (modifies *home*)

Did you bring **your** violin? (modifies *violin*)
The dog lost **its** collar. (modifies *collar*)
We like **our** new radio. (modifies *radio*)
Do you like **my** new coat? (modifies *coat*)
The manager has **his** report. (modifies *report*)

Demonstrative and *indefinite pronouns* are also used as adjectives. Demonstrative pronouns that function as adjectives are often called **demonstrative adjectives** because they have not lost their pointing out function. In the following sentences the demonstrative pronouns are used as adjectives:

This camera belongs to Jane. (modifies *camera*)
Those apples are delicious. (modifies *apples*)
That man is an army officer. (modifies *man*)
These cards are Easter cards. (modifies *cards*)

Indefinite pronouns used as adjectives are generally regarded as pure adjectives, although they may be called **indefinite adjectives.** They have no special function. The following examples illustrate their use as adjectives:

Each girl carried a flag. (modifies *girl*)
Both men received a promotion. (modifies *men*)
Neither answer is correct. (modifies *answer*)
Many soldiers were on that ship. (modifies *soldiers*)
Any mechanic could do that job. (modifies *mechanic*)
Several tables were ruined. (modifies *tables*)

Interrogative pronouns are also often used as adjectives. Since the adjective is the word that asks the question, these adjectives are called **interrogative adjectives.** In the sentence, *Which house did you buy?* the word *which* asks the question. It is also an adjective modifying the noun *house.* Note how the pronouns are used to ask questions in the following sentences:

What newspapers does he read? (modifies *newspapers*)

50

Whose name did he call? (modifies *name*)
Which play do you like best? (modifies *play*)

POSSESSIVE FORMS OF PRONOUNS

The possessive forms of the *personal pronouns* and the possessive form of the pronoun *who* are never written with an apostrophe. These pronouns have a special form to show possession and do not require an apostrophe. The correct forms to use in order to show possession are the following: *my, mine, yours, his, hers, its, ours, theirs, whose.* Do not place an apostrophe either before or after the **s** in any of these words.

The word *it's* is a contraction of *it is.* It is not a form of the pronoun, and should never be used to show possession. The word *who's* is a contraction of *who is* or *who has*, and should not be confused with the possessive form *whose.*

Contractions

It's on my desk. (*It is* on my desk.)
Who's speaking tonight? (*Who is* speaking tonight?)
Who's finished the test? (*Who has* finished the test?)

Indefinite pronouns do not have special forms to show possession. Therefore, it is necessary to use the apostrophe to show the possessive forms of these pronouns. Since most of these pronouns are used only in the singular, the possessive is formed by adding the *apostrophe* and **s** (**'s**). The plural of the indefinite pronoun *other* is *others.* In the case of this plural form, the apostrophe is placed after the **s**. Study these forms carefully:

Possessive Forms of Indefinite Pronouns

everybody's job	*anyone's* opinions
somebody's hat	*someone's* car
one's relatives	*each one's* duty
another's problems	*others'* affairs (plural)

When *else* is added to an indefinite pronoun, it is regarded as part of the pronoun. In this case, the apostrophe and **s** are added to *else* to form the possessive.

I came home with *somebody else's* coat.
Someone else's book was substituted for mine.

7. AGREEMENT OF PRONOUN WITH ANTECEDENT

You have already learned that a pronoun usually refers to a noun or pronoun which precedes it in the sentence. The word to which the pronoun refers is called its antecedent. The word *antecedent* comes from two Latin words which mean "*going before*." The antecedent of a pronoun is the word which "*goes before*" the pronoun. It is the word to which the pronoun refers.

In the sentence, *Robert lost his fishing tackle*, the pronoun *his* refers to *Robert*. The word *Robert* precedes the pronoun *his* or "goes before" it. *Robert* is the antecedent of *his*. It is the word to which the pronoun *his* refers.

Antecedents of Pronouns

<u>Margaret</u> attended <u>her</u> class reunion. (*Margaret*—antecedent of *her*)

Every <u>day</u> brings <u>its</u> duties. (*day*—antecedent of *its*)

The <u>men</u> brought <u>their</u> golf clubs. (*men*—antecedent of *their*)

Only a <u>few</u> brought <u>their</u> equipment. (*few*—antecedent of *their*)

The <u>professor</u> <u>himself</u> did not know the answer. (*professor*—antecedent of *himself*)

AGREEMENT OF PRONOUN AND ANTECEDENT IN GENDER

Since a pronoun stands for, or replaces a noun, it must agree with that noun in person, number, and gender. We have already considered the problems of number and person in Chapters Five and Six. In this unit we shall take up the problem of gender, and show its connection with the agreement of pronoun and antecedent.

In grammar **gender** means the classification of nouns and pronouns according to distinctions in sex. There are four genders: *masculine gender, feminine gender, common gender*, and *neuter gender*.

Masculine gender denotes the male sex. **Feminine gender** denotes the female sex. **Common gender** denotes either sex. **Neuter gender** denotes absence of sex. The following are examples of nouns and pronouns in the four genders:

Masculine gender—he, him, father, kind
Feminine gender—sister, she, her, princess
Common gender—child, adult, cousin, neighbor
Neuter gender—table, book, dress, radio, it

Some nouns and a few pronouns have special forms to show gender. The following list shows the changes that occur in some words to indicate a change in the gender. Some of the distinctions formerly used to show gender are passing out of use. The words *authoress* and *poetess*, for example, are seldom used.

SPECIAL FORMS TO SHOW GENDER

Masculine	Feminine	Masculine	Feminine
uncle	aunt	god	goddess
bull	cow	aviator	aviatrix
waiter	waitress	hero	heroine
alumnus	alumna	count (title)	countess
emperor	empress	gander	goose
host	hostess	sir	madam
peacock	peahen	ram	ewe
male	female	lion	lioness
monk	nun	duke	duchess
actor	actress	nephew	niece
bachelor	spinster	prince	princess
executor	executrix	fiance	fiancee
baron	baroness	stallion	mare
he	she	father	mother
lad	lass	him	her

man	woman	boy	girl
rooster	hen	husband	wife
master	mistress	buck (stag)	doe
brother	sister	landlord	landlady
drake	duck	son	daughter

GENDER AND NUMBER OF INDEFINITE PRONOUNS

Indefinite pronouns present a problem in gender. These pronouns often refer to both sexes, masculine and feminine. When we say, *Everybody went to the game,* the indefinite pronoun *everybody* includes individuals of both genders, masculine and feminine.

The problem arises when the indefinite pronoun is the antecedent of another pronoun. In that case, the accepted practice is to *use the masculine gender for the pronoun that is used in place of the indefinite pronoun.*

In the sentence, *Everyone received his income tax form,* the indefinite pronoun *everyone* is the antecedent of the pronoun *his.* It is the word to which the pronoun *his* refers. Although *everyone* includes persons of both genders, the masculine pronoun *his* is used instead of saying *his or her* income tax form.

If the sentence shows clearly that the indefinite pronoun refers to members of only one sex, the pronoun that refers to that sex should be used.

Everyone attending the meeting of the Women's Athletic Club presented **her** membership card.

In this sentence the members are women, and the pronoun *her* is used correctly. In cases where it is not clear whether the antecedent is masculine or feminine, use the pronoun *his.*

Anyone may have **his** money refunded.
Somebody left **his** pen on my desk.

Indefinite pronouns also present a problem in number. Some of them are always singular. Some are always plural, and some may be either singular or plural.

Pronouns That Are Always Singular

The following pronouns are always singular. A pronoun that is used in place of one of these indefinite pronouns must also be singular.

anybody	everybody	neither
anyone	everyone	one
another	many a one	other
each	nobody	someone
either	no one	somebody

Study the following illustrations carefully. These sentences show the proper agreement between pronoun and antecedent when the antecedent is singular.

Neither of the men had **his** tools. (not *their*)
If **anyone** wants a pen, **he** can obtain one here. (not *they*)
One likes to do what **he** can do well. (not *they*)
Someone left **his** coat in **his** locker. (not *their*)

Pronouns That Are Always Plural

The following pronouns are always plural. A pronoun that is used in place of one of them must also be plural.

many	both	few	several	others

Notice that *many a one* is included in the list of pronouns that are always singular, whereas *many* is included in this plural list. When singular expressions, such as *a man, a one, a person*, etc., are added to *many,* the *pronoun* is singular, not plural.

Several found **their** cars unlocked. (*Several*—plural)
Only a **few** would sacrifice **their** savings. (*few*—plural)
Many brought **their** lunches with them. (*Many*—plural)

Others found **their** friends in the balcony. (*Others*—plural)

Pronouns That May Be Either
Singular or Plural

The pronouns *all*, *any*, *some*, and *none* are singular or plural according to the meaning of the sentence. When these pronouns refer to **number,** they are generally regarded as plural. When they refer to **quantity** or to a **mass,** they are regarded as singular.

The pronoun *none* is singular when it clearly means *no one*, or *not one*. It is often difficult to determine the number of this pronoun since there are sentences in which it carries a plural idea. If you want to express the singular idea use *no one*, or *not one*.

Some found **their** children in the park. (*Some* is plural.)

Some of the candy has lost **its** flavor. (*Some* is singular.)

All were waiting for **their** salary checks. (*All* is plural.)

There is no candy in the box. **All** of **it** has been eaten. (*All* is singular.)

Did **any** of the men have **their** membership cards? (*Any* is plural.)

None have arrived. (*None*—plural in use)

None of these is a typical example. (*None*—singular in use)

AGREEMENT OF THE PRONOUN
WITH A COMPOUND ANTECEDENT

Sometimes the pronoun refers to two antecedents connected by *and*. If both of these antecedents are singular and refer to *different persons or things*, the antecedent is plural. The pronoun that refers to these antecedents must also be plural.

The <u>president</u> and <u>the manager</u> have outlined <u>their</u> plans.

If the antecedent refers to *one* person who fulfills *two* functions, the pronoun that takes the place of the antecedent is singular. In the following sentence *cook* and *housekeeper* are the same person.

The <u>cook and housekeeper</u> did not like her duties.

If the housekeeper were another individual, the word *the* would be placed before the word *housekeeper*.

The <u>cook</u> and <u>the housekeeper</u> did not like <u>their</u> duties.

When the connectives, *either—or* and *neither—nor* join singular nouns, the antecedent is singular. When they join plural nouns, the antecedent is plural. When they join nouns that differ in number, the pronoun should agree with the antecedent that is nearer to it.

Either *Jane* or *Alice* left **her** book on **her** desk.
(Nouns are singular—pronoun is singular)

Either the *boys* or the *girls* left **their** books on the table.
(Both nouns are plural—pronoun is plural)

Neither *Harvey* nor his *cousins* wore **their** dress suits.
(Pronoun is plural—agrees with cousins)

Neither the *men* nor the *boy* could find **his** place in the line.
(Pronoun agrees with *boy* which is nearer to it.)

In sentences like the last one, it is better to place the plural noun nearer to the pronoun. By doing so, you make the antecedent plural, and the sentence sounds better.

AGREEMENT OF PRONOUN WITH COLLECTIVE NOUNS

Collective nouns are singular when they designate a group *acting as a unit*. They are plural when the members who make up the group are *acting independently*. The pronoun that takes the place of the collective noun must agree with it in number. If the collective noun expresses a singular idea, the pronoun is singular. If the collective noun expresses a plural idea, the pronoun is plural.

The <u>band</u> played <u>its</u> fifth concert. (*acting as a unit*)
The <u>band</u> were tuning up <u>their</u> instruments. (*as individuals*)

You can readily see that the second sentence could not refer to the band as a unit. That would mean that the members of the band were all working on the same instrument.

AGREEMENT OF PRONOUN AND ANTECEDENT IN PERSON

A pronoun must agree with its antecedent in **person.** If the antecedent of the pronoun is in the *third person,* the pronoun that refers to it must also be in the *third person*. If the antecedent is in the *second person*, the pronoun should be in the *second person*.

One of the most common mistakes in English is to start the sentence in the *third person* and then put the pronoun that refers to the antecedent in the *second person*. Study the following examples carefully:

If <u>anybody</u> wants an education, <u>you</u> can get it. (*incorrect*)
If <u>anybody</u> wants an education, <u>he</u> can get it. (*correct*)
When <u>one</u> pays attention, <u>you</u> learn better. (*incorrect*)
When <u>one</u> pays attention, <u>he</u> (or *one*) learns better. (*correct*)

VAGUE ANTECEDENTS

A pronoun should not have two possible antecedents in the same sentence. If it is not clear which of two nouns a pronoun refers to, there will be two possible interpretations of the sentence. Observe the two possible interpretations in the following illustration:

James told his friend that **he** had been elected president.

In this sentence, does the pronoun *he* refer to *James* or to *friend?* If the antecedent of the pronoun *he* is *friend,* the sentence means that *James told his friend that he (the friend) had been elected president.* If the antecedent of the pronoun *he* is *James,* the sentence means that *James told his friend that he (James) had been elected president.*

The sentence might be rewritten in either of the two following ways, since we do not know which meaning the author intended:

James said to his friend, "You have been elected president."
James said to his friend, "I have been elected president."

Many of the errors that are made in the use of pronouns are caused by a lack of agreement between pronoun and antecedent. The pronoun should refer definitely to the noun which it represents. In the following sentence, to what does the pronoun *it* refer?

Your letter and your check arrived promptly, but we cannot ship **it** at present.

There is no antecedent for the pronoun *it* in the sentence. Neither the word *letter* nor the word *check* could be the antecedent. *It* probably refers to an order for goods which was included in the letter. If the word *it* refers to an order for goods, the sentence might be written as follows:

Your letter and your check arrived promptly, but at present we cannot ship the goods ordered.

ADJECTIVE—PRONOUN AGREEMENT

Demonstrative adjectives should agree in *number* with the nouns they modify. The adjectives *this, that, these,* and *those* sometimes cause agreement trouble when they modify such nouns as *kind, sort, type,* and *variety.*

Keep in mind that the demonstrative adjectives *this* and *that* are singular and should be used only with singular nouns. *These* and *those* are plural and should be used only with the plural nouns.

these kind of apples **(incorrect)**
this kind of apples (or apple) **(correct)**
or **these kinds** of apples (plural)

those sort of roses **(incorrect)**
that sort of roses (or rose) **(correct)**
or **those sorts** of roses (plural)

these variety of fruits **(incorrect)**
this variety of fruits or fruit **(correct)**
or **these varieties** of fruits (plural)

The forms in italic are incorrect because the adjective does not agree with the noun in number. The forms in bold face are correct because the adjective agrees with the noun in number.

8. COMPLEMENTS OF VERBS
THE DIRECT OBJECT

Every sentence must have a basic structure in order to express a complete thought. This basic structure may consist of only two parts, a subject noun or pronoun and a predicate verb or verb phrase. Many sentences require a third part or an additional word in order to express a complete thought. This additional word or group of words is necessary to complete the idea expressed by the verb.

The group of words, *The men lifted,* contains a subject noun *men* and a predicate verb *lifted.* Still it does not express a complete thought. A word is needed to tell **what** the men lifted. The sentence might be completed by adding the word *beam.* The completed sentence, *The men lifted the beam,* expresses a complete thought.

The word *beam* completes the meaning expressed by the verb *lifted.* For that reason it is called a **complement** or a completing word. The three essential parts of this sentence are the **subject,** the **verb,** and the **complement.** The complement is *beam.*

A complement completes the meaning expressed by a verb. The *complement* of a verb that expresses *action* is called the **direct object** of the verb. A direct object usually answers the questions *what?* or *whom?* In the preceding sentence the verb *lifted* expresses action. The complement *beam* tells *what* the men lifted. Notice how the underlined complements in the following sentences complete the meaning of the verb.

I saw Evelyn at the convention.

    (*Evelyn* tells whom I saw.)

The engineer stopped the train.

    (*Train* tells what he stopped.)

The sailors saluted the captain.

    (tells *whom* they saluted)

She refused the invitation.

(tells *what* she refused)

Some verbs that express action are complete without the addition of a complement. When such verbs are used in sentences, only two parts are essential—the *subject* and the *verb*.

Study the following illustrations. You will readily see that the thought is complete without the addition of a complement.

Jane is singing.
We have been studying.
The boys are playing.

Although the verbs in the preceding sentences do not require a complement or a completing word, a complement might be added to some of them to make the meaning more explicit. The underlined words are complements and are called *direct objects*.

Jane is singing a ballad.

(tells *what* Jane is singing)

We have been studying Spanish.

(tells *what* we have been studying)

The boys are playing games.

(tells *what* the boys are playing)

The **direct object** of a verb names the *receiver* of the action. It completes the meaning of the verb. A direct object is usually a noun or a pronoun. Adjectives and adverbs are never used as direct objects. Adjectives and adverbs are always used as modifiers. If you have any difficulty in deciding which word is the direct object, apply this test: Find the word that answers the question *what?* or *whom?* Apply the test in the following sentences:

The farmer planted the **seeds** in rows.

What did the farmer plant? The answer is, "He planted the *seeds.*" The word *seeds* is the direct object of the verb planted. It tells **what** he planted.

I met *Uncle Henry* in the bank.

Whom did I meet? The answer is, "I met Uncle Henry." The direct object is *Uncle Henry.* It tells **whom** I met.

A verb may take two or more direct objects. In this case, the verb or verb phrase has a compound object.

He grows *orchids* and *lilies* in his garden.

I met *Jerry* and *Jane* at the stadium.

TRANSITIVE AND INTRANSITIVE VERBS

When an action verb takes a direct object, it is called a **transitive verb.** The word *transitive* comes from two Latin words which mean *"passing across."* When the verb is transitive, the action passes across from a **doer** (the subject) to a **receiver** of the action (the direct object). When we say that a verb is *transitive*, it is the same as saying that it has a *direct object*.

Any verb that does not take a direct object is **intransitive.** That is, the verb does *not* express action that passes over to a receiver.

A verb may be transitive in one sentence and intransitive in another sentence. The verb may express action, but the action may not pass over to a receiver. In that case the verb is intransitive. When the verb is transitive, it always takes a direct object—the receiver of the action.

The following sentences show the same verb used as a *transitive* verb with a direct object (underlined) in the first sentence and as an *intransitive* verb with no object in the second sentence:

The sexton rang the bell.
  The bell rang loudly. (*no object*)

The ship sailed the seas.
  The ship sails at noon. (*no object*)

I met my friend at the airport.
  The delegates met yesterday. (*no object*)

THE INDIRECT OBJECT

Some verbs that express action take two objects, a direct object and an indirect object. The **indirect object** tells *to whom* the action is directed or *for whom* the action is performed.

The indirect object is used after certain verbs: *get, give, lend, offer, read, tell, buy, send, show, make, pay,* etc.

In the sentence, *Mother bought Ellen a coat*, there are two objects, a direct object and an indirect object. The word *coat* is the direct *object*. It tells *what* Mother bought. The word *Ellen* is the indirect object. It tells *for whom* Mother bought a coat. The indirect object *always* precedes or comes before the direct object. In the following sentences the indirect object and the direct object are underlined.

The librarian read the children a story.
Give him five dollars for his services.
The tailor made Edward a brown suit.

There are two tests that you can apply in order to identify an indirect object. One test is to determine the position of the object. *The indirect object always precedes the direct object.* The other test is to determine whether the indirect object seems to be the object of the preposition *to* or *for* understood. The following sentences illustrate this point:

The librarian read **(to)** the children a story.

Give **(to)** him five dollars for his services.
The tailor made **(for)** Edward a brown suit.

The words *to* and *for* are never expressed when a word functions as an indirect object. If we change the order of the sentence and supply the preposition, our sentence would read as follows: *The librarian read a story to the children.* In this sentence the word *children* is no longer the indirect object but is the object of the preposition *to*.

LINKING VERBS

Most verbs describe or express action. However, there are a small group that do not. The verb **to be** is the most important verb in this group. Since it is the most irregular verb in our language, you should be familiar with its various forms. The following verbs and verb phrases are forms of the verb *to be*:

Forms of the Verb "To Be"

am	will be	shall have been
are	shall be	will have been
is	have been	could have been
was	has been	would have been
were	had been	might have been
		should have been

Although the verb *to be*, as well as the other verbs belonging in this group, does not express action, it has another function in the sentence. The chief purpose of this verb is to serve as a link which joins the subject to some word in the predicate that gives the meaning to the sentence. For that reason, it is called a **linking verb.**

Linking verbs have very little meaning of their own. With the help of another word, they express various ideas in regard to the subject. In the sentence, *Mary is ill*, the verb *is* (a form of *to be*) is used with the adjective *ill* to describe the condition

66

of the subject, *Mary*. The sentence really means *ill Mary*, but you need a verb in order to make a complete statement.

In the sentence, *The young man was an aviator*, the verb *was* is a linking verb. With the help of the noun *aviator*, it identifies or classifies the young man. The noun *aviator* means the same as the subject. In the sentence, *The actress is very beautiful*, the verb *is*, with the help of the adjective *beautiful*, describes the appearance of the actress.

The verbs *become* and *seem*, like the verb *to be*, are almost always used as linking verbs. The following verbs are used both as linking verbs and as action verbs. The meaning of the sentence will show to which classification they belong:

Linking and Action Verbs

grow	look	smell	remain
turn	feel	taste	keep
prove	sound	appear	stay

This group of words is important because a great many mistakes in English are made when a speaker of writer does not understand their linking function.

When these words have a linking function, they have practically the same meaning as the verb *to be* would have in the same sentence. By supplying the the verb *to be* mentally after one of these verbs, you can readily tell whether the verb has a linking function or whether it is used as an action verb. Every one of the verbs in the following sentences is a linking verb. The verb *to be* has been supplied to show you how to interpret the sentence when the verbs have a linking function.

The cookies **are** wonderful.
(wonderful cookies)
The cookies **look** (to be) delicious.
(delicious cookies)
The cookies **smell** (to be) good.
(good cookies)

67

The cookies **taste** (to be) sweet.
(sweet cookies)
The cookies **seem** (to be) brittle.
(brittle cookies)
The cookies **became** (to be) stale.
(stale cookies)
The cookies **proved** (to be) sweet.
(sweet cookies)
The cookies **feel** (to be) hard.
(hard cookies)
The cookies **stayed** (to be) fresh.
(fresh cookies)
The cookies **appear** (to be) tempting.
(tempting cookies)
The cookies **remained** (to be) soft.
(soft cookies)
The cookies **kept** (to be) fresh.
(fresh cookies)

Some of the same verbs that were used in the preceding illustrations may also be used to express action. Note the differences in meaning when these verbs function as action verbs and not as linking verbs.

John **appeared** promptly.
(made his appearance)
The horticulturist **grows** orchids.
(produces by cultivation)
I **turned** the key in the lock.
We **proved** a theorem in geometry.
The doctor **felt** the broken bone.
The warden **sounded** the gong.
The chef **tasted** the sauce.
We **kept** a record of our journey.
The dog **smelled** the meat.

The judge **will stay** the trial. (postpone)
The committee **looked** at the pictures.

COMPLEMENTS OF LINKING VERBS

A *linking verb* cannot make a complete predicate. It always requires a *complement*. The group of words, *My friend is*, does not make a complete statement. The verb *is* requires some additional word to complete the meaning of the sentence. That word may be a noun, a pronoun, or an adjective.

My friend is an <u>executive</u>.
My friend is very <u>ambitious</u>.
That is <u>he</u>.

The noun that completes the meaning of a linking verb is called a *predicate noun* because it is found in the predicate. A **predicate noun** completes the verb and renames or explains the subject. In the preceding illustration, *executive* is a predicate noun. It renames the subject *friend* and classifies *friend* as an *executive*. The noun *friend* and the noun *executive* refer to the same person.

A pronoun that follows a linking verb functions in the same way as the noun. It completes the verb and means the same person or thing as the subject. It is called a **predicate pronoun**.

An adjective that follows a linking verb is called a **predicate adjective** because it is found in the predicate. A predicate adjective always modifies the subject.

The following sentences illustrate the use of the predicate noun, predicate pronoun, and predicate adjective:

Our <u>manager</u> was a former army <u>colonel</u>.
   (*manager* and *colonel*—same person)
Our <u>manager</u> is very <u>efficient</u>.
   (*efficient* modifies *manager*)

The <u>candidate</u> for the position is <u>he</u>.
   (*he* and *candidate*—same person)

In the first sentence, *colonel* is a **predicate noun**. It completes the meaning of the verb *was* and refers to the same person as the subject. In the second sentence *efficient* is a **predicate adjective**. It modifies the subject noun *manager*. In the third sentence, *he* is a **predicate pronoun**. It means the same person as the subject *candidate*.

9. CASE OF NOUNS AND PRONOUNS

Nouns and pronouns have certain relationships to other words in a sentence. We call attention to these relationships by indicating the case of the noun or pronoun. The word **case** is used in grammar to indicate the *relationship* a noun or a pronoun has to other words in the sentence. The case of a noun or a pronoun is determined by the particular use of that noun or pronoun in the sentence.

There are only three cases in English: the *nominative case*, the *objective case*, and the *possessive case*. The **nominative case** is the case of the *subject*. The **objective case** is the case of the *object*. The **possessive case** is the case that shows *ownership*.

CASE OF NOUNS

Nouns present very few problems in case because the same form is used for the nominative case and the objective case. The only way to determine whether a noun is in the nominative case or in the objective case is to determine its relationship to other words in the sentence. If the noun is used as the *subject* of the sentence, it is in the *nominative case*. If the noun is used as the *object* of a verb or a preposition, it is in the *objective case*.

The **door** is open.

   (*nominative case*—subject)

I closed the **door.**

   (*objective case*—direct object)

In the first sentence, the noun *door* is used as the subject of the sentence. It is in the nominative case. In the second sentence, the same form *door* is used as the direct object of the verb *closed*. *Door* is in the objective case in this sentence.

Like nouns, *indefinite pronouns* have the same form for the nominative case and the objective case.

Everyone contributed five dollars.
(*nominative case*—subject)
I saw **everyone** at the game.
(*objective case*—direct object)

NOMINATIVE CASE

The word *nominative* comes from a Latin word which means *name*. The **nominative case** names the case of the subject of the sentence. It also names the case of a predicate noun. A prdicate noun is in the nominative case. For this reason, it is often called a **predicate nominative.**

A *predicate noun* must agree in case with the *subject* because it refers to the same person or thing as the subject. It also follows a verb which cannot take an object. Nouns used after linking verbs are called predicate nouns. In the following sentences the subjects and the predicate nouns are underlined.

My <u>friend</u> is a naval <u>officer</u>.
The leading <u>lady</u> was <u>Mary Harris</u>.

In the first sentence, *officer* is a prdicate noun. It is used after the linking verb is and refers to the same person as the subject. It is in the nominative case to agree with the case of the subject *friend*.

In the second sentence, *Mary Harris* is a predicate noun. It is in the nominative case to agree with the subject *lady*. *Mary Harris* and *lady* refer to the same person.

OBJECTIVE CASE

The **objective case** is the case of the *object*. The *direct object* of a verb, the *indirect object*, and the *object* of a *preposition* are in the objective case.

Lester writes **articles** for the paper.

(*articles*—direct object)

Arthur sent the **manager** a detailed report.

(*manager*—indirect object)

In the first sentence, *articles* is the direct object of the verb *writes*. It tells **what** Lester writes. *Articles* is in the objective case. In the second sentence, *manager* is the indirect object. It tells **to whom** Arthur sent his report. *Manager* is in the objective case.

In Chapter Two you learned that a preposition is always followed by some noun or pronoun which is called the *object* of the *preposition*. The object of a preposition is always in the objective case.

Edward met his lawyer at the **bank.**

(object of preposition **at**)

We met Marvin in the **lobby.**

(object of preposition **in**)

In the first sentence, the preposition *at* is followed by the noun *bank*. The object of the preposition is *bank,* which is in the objective case. In the second sentence, *lobby* is the object of the preposition *in*. *Lobby* is in the objective case.

It is easy to remember that direct objects of verbs, indirect objects of verbs, and objects of prepositions are in the objective case because they are all called **objects** of some type. The fact that they are objects indicates that they are in the **objective case.**

CASE OF PRONOUNS

Nouns do not present any problems in case because the form of the noun is the same for the nominative case and the objective case. Pronouns do present problems in case. The *personal pronouns* and the pronoun *who* have different forms to indicate the different cases.

There are only *six pronouns* in English that have these special forms to show *case*, but the changes that occur to indicate case are very important. They are responsible for many of the errors that frequently occur in the use of pronouns. You should become familiar with the different forms of these pronouns, and you should learn how to use them correctly. The six pronouns are *I, you, he, she, it, who*. The following table gives the nominative case forms and the objective case forms of each of the six pronouns:

Nominative Case		Objective Case	
Singular	**Plural**	**Singular**	**Plural**
I	we	me	us
you	you	you	you
he	they	him	them
she	they	her	them
it	they	it	them
who	who	whom	whom

The pronouns *he, she,* and *it* all have the same plural form. *They* is the pronoun used in the nominative case in the plural for each of the three pronouns. *Them* is the pronoun used in the objective case in the plural for each of the three pronouns.

NOMINATIVE CASE OF PRONOUNS

Like nouns, pronouns are in the nominative case when they are used as the subjects of sentences, or as predicate pronouns after one of the linking verbs. Mistakes are seldom made in selecting the correct from of the pronoun to use as the subject of the sentence. Mistakes are frequently made, however, when a pronoun is used as a *predicate nominative*. The following sentences illustrate the correct use of the six pronouns in the nominative case:

Subject of the Sentence	Predicate Pronoun
I saw the accident.	It is **I.**
You have been elected.	It is **you.**
He attended the lecture.	It might be **he.**
She gave me her note book.	It could **she**.
It is my overcoat.	Could this be **it?**
We are great friends. (plural)	It is **we.**
They arrived early.	It was **they.**
(Plural)	(plural)
Who came in?	**Who** was it?
	(It was **who?**)

The pronoun *you* does not present any problem in the plural, because the forms for the plural are the same as the forms for the singular. The form of the pronoun *you* is also the same for the nominative case and the objective case.

Interrogative sentences should always be transposed and put in normal order. When this is done, it is easy to determine the case of the pronoun.

OBJECTIVE CASE OF PRONOUNS

Pronouns are in the objective case when they are used as direct objects of verbs, or as objects of prepositions. The correct forms to use in the objective case are *me, you, him, her, it,* and *whom* in the singular, and *us, you them, whom* in the plural. The following sentences illustrate the correct use of these pronouns in the objective case:

Object of the Verb

Mother called **me.**
Jack saw **him** yesterday.
I met **you** in Paris.
The firm sent **her** to Texas.
My friend invited **us** to the game.

75

Sue drove **them** to the station.
Whom did you call?

Indirect Object of the Verb

Ethel gave **me** her pen.
I sent **him** a notice.
David sent **you** a ticket.
Jack offered **her** a seat.
The tailor made **us** new uniforms.
The teacher read **them** a story.

Object of a Preposition

The telegram was sent to **me**. (object of the preposition *to*)
The manager created the position for **him**. (object of *for*)
The author wrote an article about **us**. (object of *about*)
The waiter placed their table near **us**. (object of *near*)
We distributed the gifts among **them**. (object of *among*)

THE POSSESSIVE CASE OF NOUNS

The **possessive case** shows *ownership* or *possession*. The use of the possessive case does not present much of a problem in speaking, but it does present a problem in writing and spelling. Although the rule for forming the possessive case of nouns is very simple, many persons have considerable difficulty in spelling and writing the forms correctly.

One simple rule applies to all cases: If the singular form of the noun does not end in **s**, add the *apostrophe* and **s** (**'s**). If the singular ends in **s**, add the *apostrophe* (**'**). Study the following examples carefully and try to apply the rule:

Singular		Plural	
boy	boy's	boys	boys'
lady	lady's	ladies	ladies'
hero	hero's	heroes	heroes'
man	man's	men	men's
Charles	Charles'	Charleses	Charleses'
child	child's	children	children's

There is one fact that you must always keep in mind in order to form the possessive case correctly; that is, the sign of the possessive is something that is *added* to the word. It is not something that is inserted within the word. You must be absolutely sure of the correct form for the singular and the correct form for the plural before you add the sign of the possessive.

Take the proper name, *Dickens*, for example. This is a proper noun in the singular which ends in **s**. The sign of the possessive must be added to the complete word and not inserted within the word. The possessive form is often incorrectly written as *Dicken's*. That would be the possessive form of the name *Dicken*, and not the possessive form of the name *Dickens*. The singular possessive form of *Dickens* is *Dickens'* as shown below:

Oliver Twist is one of **Dicken's** novels. (incorrect)
Oliver Twist is one of **Dickens'** novels. (correct)

The possessive forms of proper nouns are formed according to the rule. If the singular form of the name does not end in **s**, add the *apostrophe* and **s**. If the singular ends in **s**, add the *apostrophe*. The same rule applies to the plural.

Singular		**Plural**	
Mary	Mary's	Marys	Marys'
Jones	Jones'	Joneses	Joneses'
Henry	Henry's	Henrys	Henrys'
Burns	Burns'	Burnses	Burnses'

There is one slight modification of the rule which may be followed in the case of the possessive singular of nouns that end in **s**. If you want the sound of the additional **s**, the *apostrophe* and **s** may be added

This is **Charles'** fishing rod. (correct)
This is **Charles's** fishing rod. (correct)
I saw **Doris'** picture at the studio. (correct)

I saw **Doris's** picture at the studio. (correct)

In modern practice, the first form (*Charles' fishing rod*) is the form that is generally used. It follows the rule given, and is the simpler form to use in writing and in pronunciation. This rule also applies to nouns ending in **x** and **z**.

I bought a jar of **Heinz'** pickles. (correct)
She has always worn **Knox'** hats. (correct)
I bought a jar of **Heinz's** pickles. (correct)
She has always worn **Knox's** hats. (correct)

USE OF THE POSSESSIVE —SPECIAL FORMS

As a rule, it is better practice not to use the possessive forms for inanimate objects. Inanimate objects cannot possess anything in the sense that animate objects can. Avoid expressions such as *the table's top*, *the book's ending*, *the lake's shore*, and *the shop's window*. It is much better to use the phrase with *of* in such cases.

the top **of the table**   the shore **of the lake**
the ending **of the book**   the window **of the shop**

There are certain exceptions to this rule. Usage has established authority for using expressions such as the following:

the earth's surface   the sun's rays
the world's progress   today's edition
the law's delay   time's flight
the season's greetings   the water's edge

Certain expressions relating to *time*, *distance*, and *value* are also written with the sign of the possessive case. The apostrophe is generally used in expressions like the following:

78

a moment's delay   a stone's throw
two weeks' salary   a week's journey
a month's vacation   ten cents' worth
a few minutes' quiet   thirty days' notice

The singular possessive and the plural possessive of compound nouns are formed by adding the sign of the possessive to the end of the compound word.

Singular	**Plural**
sister-in-law's	sisters-in-law's
editor-in-chief's	editors-in-chief's
maid of honor's	maids of honor's

Joint ownership is shown by making the last word in the series possessive. Individual ownership is shown by making both parts possessive.

Baker and Johnson's factory. (joint ownership)
Baker's and Johnson's factories. (individual ownership)

Asia and China's problems. (common to both)
Asia's and China's problems. (separate problems)

Some trade names and names of organizations and institutions are written with the sign of the possessive case, and some are not. In writing letters, one should follow the form established by the organization.

When the apostrophe and **s** ('**s**) are not used, the word which would ordinarily be written as a possessive is regarded as an adjective modifier. In the name of an institution, such as *Teachers College*, the apostrophe is not used. The word *Teachers* is regarded as an adjective modifying *College*. It tells the type of college. It does not mean that the teachers possess the college.

The following illustrations show the methods used in writing place names, institutional names, and titles of publications:

With the Apostrophe	Without the Apostrophe
Harper's Magazine	Womens Athletic Club
Hansen's Pharmacy	Bricklayers Union
Queen's College (Oxford)	Executives Club
Charles Scribner's Sons	Pikes Peak
Young Men's Christian Association	Downers Grove
Working Girl's Club	Harris Brothers Company
Illinois Children's Home and Aid Society	Citizens League
Nowak's Optical Service	American Bankers Association
Ladies' Home Journal	Buzzards Bay
Martha's Vineyard Island	Peoples Finance Company

THE POSSESSIVE CASE OF PRONOUNS

The indefinite pronouns do not have special forms to show case. The possessive case of indefinite pronouns is formed in the same way as the possessive case of nouns. Indefinite pronouns are seldom used in the plural. Two of the indefinite pronouns, *one* and *other*, have the plural forms *ones* and *others*. The following are illustrations of the possessive case form of indefinite pronouns:

everyone's opinion   *one's* relatives (singular)
someone's hat   *somebody's* car
anybody's guess   *another's* choice

The *personal pronouns* and the pronoun *who* have special forms to show the possessive case: *my, mine, our, ours, your, yours, her, hers, his, its, their, theirs,* and *whose*. These forms are never written with an apostrophe. To add an apostrophe would be adding a possessive sign to a word that is already possessive.

Whose report did you check? (not *Who's*)
The automobile was **theirs**. (not *their's*)
I did not know that book was **yours**. (not *your's*)
The ship lost **its** anchor in the storm. (not *it's*)
That ranch type house is **ours**. (not *our's*)

PERSONAL PRONOUNS

Singular and Plural

First Person

Nominative	I
	we
Possessive	my, mine
	our, ours
Objective	me
	us

Second Person

Nominative	you
	you
Possessive	your, yours
	your, yours
Objective	you
	you

Third Person

Nominative	he she it
	they
Possessive	his her, hers its
	their, theirs
Objective	you
	you

RELATIVE AND INTERROGATIVE PRONOUN "WHO"

Singular and Plural

Nominative	who
Possessive	whose
Objective	whom

10. MODIFIERS: ADJECTIVES

Adjectives give life and color to language. They also help us give more exact pictures of what we are telling about, if we know how to select them carefully. As you improve your skill in using these words, your language will become more interesting and more explicit.

Let us assume that you were telling someone about a man whom you had seen. You might start out with a sentence like this: "I met a man walking down the street." This sentence does not give us an interesting description or very accurate information. It tells very little about the man, his manner of walking, or the street down which he walked.

Someone who has skill in selecting words that would give a more definite and colorful description might change the sentence into something like this:

I met a **weary** and **disheartened old** man hobbling down the **narrow, winding** street.

This sentence has been made more colorful and more accurate by the use of the adjectives *weary, disheartened,* and *old* to describe the man, and by the use of the adjectives *narrow* and *winding* to describe the street.

In order to use adjectives effectively, you must know the exact shade of meaning that you wish to convey. Then you must be able to select the adjective or adjectives that express that shade of meaning.

You might want to use an adjective to describe a certain type of individual, and you are not sure whether to use the adjective *sly* or the adjective *cunning*. Whenever you are in doubt, consult a reliable, up-to-date dictionary. In most dictionaries these differences in meaning are pointed out.

The adjective *sly* always implies that the individual is working or acting secretly, or is using underhand methods. The adjective *cunning* implies the use of intelligence, skill, or ingenuity. The two words do not mean exactly the same thing.

The following exercise will give you excellent practice in learning how to select the adjective that expresses the exact meaning you would like to convey. The adjectives listed below are divided into groups of three. Each adjective in a group of three expresses a different shade of meaning. Try to write sentences using these words. Be sure that your sentences show the differences in meaning. The dictionary will be a great help.

1. small—diminutive—little
2. funny—strange—queer
3. strong—robust—sturdy
4. beautiful—handsome—lovely
5. bright—shining—brilliant

"OVERWORKED" ADJECTIVES

There is a tendency on the part of many people to use the same adjective to apply to a number of different situations. When a person does this, the assumption is that he has a very limited vocabulary. As a result, he is not able to express his meaning precisely. For example, he may use the word *lovely* to describe many different things. In certain cases, the adjective *lovely* is appropriate. In other cases, it is not the most appropriate or the most precise word to use. Study the following illustrations.

a *lovely* time	a *lovely* view
a *lovely* dress	a *lovely* voice
a *lovely* picnic	a *lovely* program
a *lovely* picture	a *lovely* day
a *lovely* street	a *lovely* necktie

If you wanted to describe a dress, instead of using the word *lovely*, you might use any one of the following adjectives: *becoming, stylish, fashionable, smart, colorful, modish, dashing, beautiful*, etc. The careful speaker or writer would choose the one that expressed the most exact shade of meaning he wished to convey. This requires careful analysis, but it is worth the effort.

Adjectives that are applied in many different types of situations are often called "overworked" or "shopworn" adjectives. The following adjectives belong in this list:

fine	lovely	swell
grand	nice	adorable
funny	terrible	keen
awful	crazy	sweet

KINDS OF ADJECTIVES

There are two kinds of adjectives: *descriptive* adjectives and *limiting* adjectives. **Descriptive adjectives,** as the name implies, give color and vividness to the persons, places, or things we talk or write about. **Limiting adjectives** indicate number or quantity.

Descriptive adjectives tell *what kind, what color, what size, what shape,* etc. Limiting adjectives tell *how many, how much, which one, whose,* etc.

three checks
  (limiting)
high mountain
  (descriptive)
a **new** car
  (descriptive)
two branches
  (limiting)

brilliant speaker
  (descriptive)
one airplane
  (limiting)
a **few** children
  (limiting)
a **sympathetic** listener
  (descriptive)

Adjectives derived from proper nouns are called **proper adjectives.** They are usually written with a capital letter. They are usually descriptive adjectives.

Canadian bacon
American industries
Mexican pottery
United States flag
English wool

Turkish tobacco
Norwegian sardines
Danish silver
Swedish crystal
Indian summer

PREDICATE ADJECTIVES

Adjectives that complete the meaning of the verb and modify the subject are called **predicate adjectives.** If an adjective is found in the predicate and modifies a noun in the predicate, it is not a predicate adjective. The adjective must follow a linking verb and modify the subject in order to be classified as a predicate adjective. The predicate adjective usually *describes* the subject noun or pronoun.

The list of linking verbs which was given in Chapter Eight is repeated here for reference. You should become familiar with this important list of verbs. It will help you identify the predicate adjectives that are used after linking verbs.

Linking Verbs

is	grow	look	smell	remain
become	turn	feel	taste	keep
seem	prove	sound	appear	stay

Illustrations

The predicate adjectives are underlined in the following sentences.

The cookies are <u>delicious.</u> (*delicious* cookies)

Corn is <u>plentiful</u> in Illinois. (*plentiful* corn)

The street has become very <u>muddy.</u> (*muddy* street)

Position of the Adjective

An adjective is usually placed directly before the noun it modifies. Sometimes the adjective follows the word it modifies. The predicate adjective is always found in the predicate after the verb it completes.

1. Adjectives placed before the noun.
   An **old, gnarled** tree lay across the stream.
2. Adjectives placed after the noun.
   A tree, **old** and **gnarled,** lay across the stream.

3. Predicate adjectives, placed after the verb.
   The tree was **old** and **gnarled.**

NOUNS USED AS ADJECTIVES

The use of pronouns as adjectives was explained in Chapter Six. Nouns are also frequently *used as adjectives*. The nouns in the following expressions are used as adjectives:

college credits (modifies *credits*)
dress accessories (modifies *accessories*)
window sash (modifies *sash*)
Fourth of July speech (modifies *speech*)
summer clothes (modifies *clothes*)
table lamp (modifies *lamp*)

A noun in the *possessive case* is often placed before another noun which it modifies. In such cases, the noun in the possessive case is used as an adjective although it has not lost the function of showing ownership or possession. Nouns used in this way are sometimes called **possessive adjectives.** Sometimes they are described as nouns in the possessive case used as adjectives. Observe how nouns in the possessive case are used in the following sentences:

John's car was wrecked in the crash. (*John's* modifies *car*.)
I like to shop in **Macy's** store. (*Macy's* modifies *store*.)
I am wearing my **sister's** coat. (*sister's* modifies *coat*.)

COMPARISON OF ADJECTIVES

The form of an adjective is often changed to show the extent or degree to which a certain quality is present. In grammar, this change in form to show a difference in degree is called *comparison*.

There are three degrees of comparison in English: the *positive degree*, the *comparative degree*, and the *superlative degree*.

The **positive degree** is really not a degree of comparison because no comparison is indicated when the positive degree is used. The positive degree is the simple form of the adjective. It shows that the quality is present, but it does not show a comparison with anything else. The adjectives in the following sentences are all positive degree:

That is a **beautiful** rose.
It is a very **cold** day.
Peter is very **energetic.**
Jane is **studious.**
The **old** house was sold.
It was a very **warm** day.

In the preceding illustrations, the adjective simply shows that the quality is present. No comparison is made with any other person or thing.

The **comparative degree** of the adjective is used when a comparison *is* made between **two** persons or things. The comparative degree shows that the quality expressed by the adjective exists to a *greater* or to a *lesser* degree in one of the two persons or things that are being compared.

The comparative degree of almost all adjectives of *one* syllable is formed by adding **er** to the positive degree, or to the simple form of the adjective; for example, *colder, smoother, longer, greater, stronger, firmer, thicker,* etc.

John is **stronger** than Michael. (*two persons* compared)

This table is **larger** than that table. (*two objects* compared)

In the first sentence, *two persons* are compared as to strength. According to the sentence, John possesses this quality of strength to a greater degree than Michael. The comparative degree of the adjective is used because a comparison is made between *two* persons.

88

In the second sentence, *two tables* are being compared as to size. The comparative degree of the adjective *large* is used because a comparison is made between *two objects*.

The **superlative degree** of the adjective is used when **more than two** persons or things are compared. The superlative degree indicates that the quality (expressed by the adjective) is possessed to the *greatest* or to the *least* degree by one of the persons or things included in the comparison.

Our house is the **largest** house in the block. (More than two are compared.)

Louis is the **smallest** boy in his class. (More than two are compared.)

In the first sentence, *more than two* houses are being compared. The superlative degree of the adjective *large* is used to show this fact. The house that possesses the quality expressed by the adjective *large* to the greatest degree is *our* house. It is the *largest* house in a block which contains more than two houses.

In the second sentence, more than two boys are being compared as to size. Louis possesses this quality to the *least* degree. The superlative degree of the adjective *small* is used to show this fact.

DEGREES OF COMPARISON
Adjectives of One Syllable

Positive	Comparative	Superlative
neat	neater	neatest
sharp	sharper	sharpest
dark	darker	darkest
keen	keener	keenest
long	longer	longest

Adjectives of *two or more syllables* are usually compared by prefixing the words *more* and *most* to the simple form of the adjective. *More* is used to indicate the comparison between two persons or things. *Most* is used to indicate the comparison between more than two persons or things. *Less* and *least* are used in a similar way.

Positive	Comparative	Superlative
fragrant	*more* fragrant	*most* fragrant
famous	*less* famous	*least* famous
precious	*more* precious	*most* precious
difficult	*less* difficult	*least* difficult

Sometimes adjectives of *one syllable* are compared by prefixing *more* and *most*. Sometimes adjectives of *more than one syllable* are compared by adding **er** and **est**. There is no rule to follow for making these exceptions. It is usually a matter of sound. If one form of comparison sounds better than the other, that is the form of comparison to use. It sounds better to say *crisp, more crisp, most crisp,* than to say *crisp, crisper, crispest.* Therefore, the comparison with *more* and *most* is preferred.

Adjectives of more than one syllable that end in **y** are usually compared by adding **er** and **est**. Notice the change in spelling in the comparative and in the superlative degrees. The **y** changes to **i** before the addition of **er** or **est**.

Positive	Comparative	Superlative
silly	sillier	silliest
dainty	daintier	daintiest
clumsy	clumsier	clumsiest
handy	handier	handiest
noisy	noisier	noisiest

IRREGULAR COMPARISON OF ADJECTIVES

Some adjectives are compared *irregularly*. The forms for the comparative degree and for the superlative degree usually show a marked change in the form of the word; for example, *many*, *more*, *most*. You should be familiar with these changes in order to use the correct forms for the comparative and superlative degrees.

Adjectives Compared Irregularly

Positive	Comparative	Superlative
far	worse	worst
far	further	furthest
far	farther	farthest
good, well	better	best
little	less	least
many	more	most
much	more	most
out	outer	outmost or outermost

Farther refers to *distance* or remoteness in space. **Further** refers to remoteness in *time*, to *degree, extent,* or *quantity*. It is also used to express the idea of something *more* or *additional*.

The garage is **farther** than I thought. (distance in space)
I shall give you **further** instructions tomorrow. (*additional* instructions)

The distinctions between *farther* and *further* are passing out of use. These words are now used interchangeably. There is also a tendency to use *further* to express all the meanings discussed. (See latest dictionaries.)

ADJECTIVES NOT COMPARED

There are a number of adjectives that should not be compared because the **simple** form of the adjective expresses the quality to the highest possible degree. For example, if an answer to a problem is *correct*, another answer could not possibly be *more correct*. If a circle is absolutely *round*, another circle could

91

not be *more round*. If a bottle is *empty*, another bottle could not be *more empty*.

The following are some of the adjectives that are not compared for the reasons given:

perfect	unique	square	universal
single	supreme	fatal	empty
vertical	full	alone	dead
final	mortal	round	deadly
straight	blind	everlasting	wrong

The expression, *more nearly round*, is often used when comparing two things, one of which is *more nearly round* than the other. In this case, however, neither of the things compared is round. A line could be *more nearly straight* than another line if neither of the lines was absolutely straight.

Sometimes an adjective such as the word *honest* is used in the comparative and superlative degrees. In such cases, we have no standard of absolute honesty. What the writer or speaker means is that one person approaches the absolute state of honesty to a greater or to a lesser degree than another person. The adjective *perfect* is often used in the same way.

11. MODIFIERS: ADVERBS

Chapter Two explained the uses of the adverb as a modifier of the verb, telling *how, when, where,* and *to what degree* the action is performed. This unit presents other uses of the adverb, and the relation of adverbs to adjectives and to other adverbs.

FORMS OF ADVERBS

Some people have the idea that all adverbs end in **ly.** There are a great many adverbs that do end in **ly,** but there are probably just as many that do not end in **ly.** Many adverbs are formed by adding **ly** to the adjective form:

Adjective	Adverb	Adjective	Adverb
strange	strangely	awkward	awkwardly
sudden	suddenly	necessary	necessarily
calm	calmly	strict	strictly
sure	surely	forcible	forcibly
usual	usually	extreme	extremely
swift	swiftly	similar	similarly
rapid	rapidly	slight	slightly

The following are some of the adverbs that do not end in **ly:**

seldom	little	why	fast
again	here	now	twice
soon	there	then	too
very	rather	since	much
almost	often	well	quite
late	when	near	yonder
hard	where	far	how

Many adjectives end in **ly.** They should not be confused with adverbs that end in **ly.** The following words ending in **ly** are commonly used as adjectives. Some of them might also be used as adverbs:

| stately | lovely | saintly | manly |
| lonely | womanly | lively | courtly |

Some adjectives have the same form as the adverb. In such cases, the only way you can tell whether the word is an *adjective* or an *adverb*, is to determine its use in a particular sentence. Study the following illustrations carefully:

That was a **hard** task. (*hard* adjective, modifies *task*)
Our janitor works **hard**. (*hard* adverb, modifies *works*)
We arrived at the airport **early**. (*early* adverb, modifies *arrived*)
We had to make an **early** start. (*early* adjective, modifies *start*)
That was a **cowardly** act. (*cowardly* adjective, modifies *act*)
He acted **cowardly** in that situation. (*cowardly* adverb, modifies *acted*)

INTERROGATIVE ADVERBS

An adverb is often used at the beginning of a sentence to ask a question. When an adverb is used in this way, it is called an **interrogative adverb.** An *interrogative adverb* also modifies some word in the sentence.

When did you arrive? (*When* interrogative adverb)
Where did you put my hat? (*Where* interrogative adverb)
How many books have you read? (*How* interrogative adverb)

In the first sentence, the adverb *When* asks the question. It also modifies the verb *did arrive*. (You *did arrive* when?) In the second sentence, the adverb *Where* asks the question and modifies the verb *did put*. (You *did put* my hat where?) In the third sentence, the adverb How asks the question and modifies the adjective *many*. (You have read how *many* books?)

YES, NO, AND NOT

The affirmative adverb *yes* and the negative adverb *no* are used independently. They are usually set off by commas. *Not* is an adverb. It is never used as part of the verb, although it often comes between the parts of a verb phrase. The adverb *not* makes the verb express an idea which is the exact opposite of the regular meaning of the verb.

Yes, I shall take the course.
I did *not* give him the plans. (No plans were given.)
No, we are *not* going to Florida this winter.

ADVERBS OF DEGREE

Adverbs of degree tell *how large, how small, how long, how much, to what extent*, etc. They answer the questions *"How much?" "To what extent?" "In what degree?"* Adverbs of degree usually modify adjectives or other adverbs. In the following illustrations the adverbs of degree modify *adjectives*:

This apple is very sour. (*very* modifies the adjective *sour*)
The play was rather dull. (*rather* modifies the adjective *dull*)
The price is too high. (*too* modifies the adjective *high*)

In the first sentence, the adverb of degree *very* modifies the predicate adjective *sour*. It tells to what degree the apple is sour, or how sour it is. In the second sentence, the adverb *rather* modifies the predicate adjective *dull*. It tells the extent to which the play was *dull*. In the third sentence, the adverb *too* modifies the predicate adjective *high*. It tells the extent to which the price is *high*. The adverbs *very, too*, and *rather* are commonly used as adverbs of degree.

In the following sentences, the adverbs of degree modify other *adverbs*:

The old man moved too slowly. (*too* modifies the adverb *slowly*)

John swims much faster than Ned. (*much* modifies the adverb *faster*)

Don't talk so loud. (*so* modifies the adverb *loud*)

In the first sentence, the adverb of degree too modifies the adverb *slowly*. It tells the extent to which the old man moved *slowly*. In the second sentence, the adverb of degree *much* modifies the adverb *faster*. The adverb of degree tells that John swims fast to a greater degree than Ned. In the third sentence, the adverb of degree *so* modifies the adverb *loud*. The sentence means that you should not talk loud to the extent expressed by the adverb *so*. In this sentence, the short form of the adverb (*loud*) is used instead of the longer form, *loudly*.

NOUNS USED AS ADVERBS

Nouns that express *time, size, place, measurement, degree,* or *number* are often used as adverbs. We identify these nouns by calling them *nouns used as adverbs*. Such nouns are not only used as adverbs, but they retain an important characteristic of nouns; namely, they may take an *adjective modifier*.

I am going *home*. (*home* noun used as an adverb)
Horace will arrive *Monday*. (*Monday* noun used as an adverb)
We worked all *day*. (*day* noun used as an adverb)
The fish weighed five *pounds*. (*pounds* noun used as an adverb)

In the first sentence, the noun *home* tells **where** I am going. It performs the same function as an **adverb of place.** In the second sentence, the noun *Monday* tells **when** Horace will arrive. It performs the same function as an **adverb of time.** In the third sentence, the noun *day* tells **how long** we worked, or the extent to which we worked. In the last sentence, the noun *pounds* tells the amount, or **how much** the fish weighed.

The noun *pounds* in the last sentence is modified by the adjective *five*. Although the noun *pounds* functions as an adverb, it may take an adjective modifier. It still retains that particular characteristic of a noun. It functions as two parts of speech at the same time both as a **noun** and as an **adverb.**

Some persons have difficulty in understanding the use of a noun as an adverb. A noun used as an adverb is really the equivalent of a phrase. The following illustrations will help make this clear:

I am going home. This sentence really means that I am going to *my home*. The noun *home* is the equivalent of the phrase, *to my home*.

Horace will arrive Monday. This sentence means that Horace will arrive *on Monday*. The noun *Monday* is the equivalent of the phrase, *on Monday*.

We worked all day. This sentence means that we worked for the period or to *the extent of a day*.

The fish weighed five pounds. This sentence means that the fish weighed to the extent or *to the amount of five pounds*.

COMPARISON OF ADVERBS

Adverbs are compared in exactly the same way as adjectives are compared. They have the same three degrees of comparison: the *positive degree*, the *comparative degree*, and the *superlative degree*.

A few adverbs form the comparative degree by adding **er** to the positive degree. They form the superlative degree by adding **est** to the positive degree.

Positive	Comparative	Superlative
late	later	latest
hard	harder	hardest
soon	sooner	soonest
fast	faster	fastest
near	nearer	nearest
quick (*short form*)	quicker	quickest
slow (*short form*)	slower	slowest

Most adverbs are compared by placing *more* (for the comparative degree) and *most* (for the superlative degree) before the positive forms. *Less* and *least* are used in the same way as *more* and *most*.

Positive	Comparative	Superlative
carefully	more carefully	most carefully
discreetly	more discreetly	most discreetly
abruptly	more abruptly	most abruptly
gratefully	more gratefully	most gratefully
efficiently	more efficiently	most efficiently
awkwardly	less awkwardly	least awkwardly
favorably	less favorably	least favorably
gracefully	less gracefully	least gracefully

IRREGULAR COMPARISON OF ADVERBS

A few adverbs are compared *irregularly*. In the following list you will find some words that were also in the list of adjectives that are compared irregularly. Such words are used both as *adjectives* and as *adverbs*.

Positive	Comparative	Superlative
far	farther	farthest
far	further	furthest
badly	worse	worst
little	less	least
much	more	most
well	better	best

Some adverbs are not compared. The following adverbs can not be used in the comparative or in the superlative degrees:

before	never	now	there	very	by
ever	no	so	thus	past	back
here	not	then	too	yes	whenever

The comparative degree of adverbs is used when comparing two things. The superlative degree is used when comparing more than two.

We drove *more slowly* than our guide. (Comparative)
Of the three speakers, the senator spoke *most convincingly*. (Superlative)

12. PRINCIPAL PARTS OF VERBS

Studies have shown that more than half of the errors made in English are errors in the use of verbs. Most of this trouble occurs because of confusion in the use of the principal parts.

Every verb has *three basic forms* which are called the *principal parts* of the verb. These three forms are the **present tense,** the **past tense,** and the **past participle.** They are called the principal parts of the verb because (with a few exceptions) the six tenses of the verb can be built from them.

Tense is a property that belongs to verbs. In grammar, *tense* means *time.* Every verb has certain forms which show the *time* of the *action* or the *time* of the *state of condition.* When we want to indicate that a certain action is going on now, or that a certain state of condition exists at the present time, we use the **present tense.**

Present Tense

I **drive.** (Action occurs at the *present time.*)
He **sings.** (Action occurs at the *present time.*)
Florence **is** ill. (State of condition exists at the *present time.*)

When we want to indicate that the action occurred yesterday, or in some past time, we use the **past tense** of the verb. With a few exceptions, the past tense of the verb is not the same form as the present tense of the verb.

Past Tense

I **drove.** (The action occurred in the *past.*)
He **sang** at the concert. (The action occurred in the *past.*)
Florence **was** ill yesterday. (State of condition existed in the *past.*)

In the preceding illustrations, the forms, *drive* and *sings*, are used to show that action is going on at the present time.

100

The forms, *drove* and *sang*, are used to show that action occurred at some time in the past. The forms *drive* and *sings* are the present tense of the verbs *drive* and *sing*. The forms *drove* and *sang* are the past tense of the verbs *drive* and *sing*.

The **past participle** of the verb is a verb form that is used with *have, has,* or *had* to form the perfect tenses. The past participle cannot function as the predicate verb. It is always combined with an auxiliary, such as *have, has,* or *had.* It is a part of the verb phrase.

Past Participles
I have **called** her every day this week. (*called* past participle)
We <u>have</u> **driven** there often. (*driven* past participle)

The three forms, the *present tense*, *past tense*, and the *past participle*, constitute the **principal parts** of a verb. Become familiar with the principal parts of certain verbs so that you will be able to use them correctly. The verbs that cause most of our verb troubles are the verbs that form the principal part irregularly. We shall make a special study of these verbs.

REGULAR AND IRREGULAR VERBS

Verbs are divided into two classes on the basis of the way in which the past tense and the past participle are formed. Some are called *regular* or weak verbs, and others are called *irregular* or strong verbs.

A **regular verb** is a verb that forms the past tense and the past participle by adding **ed** or **d** to the form of the present tense. Sometimes the **ed** or **d** changes to **t**: *build, built, built.*

Verb	Past Tense	Past Participle
call	called	called
bake	baked	baked
build	built	built

101

The past tense and the past participle of the verb *call* are formed by adding **ed** to the form of the present tense: *call***ed**. The past tense and the past participle of the verb *bake* are formed by simply adding **d** to the form of the present tense: *bake***d**. The past tense and the past participle of the verb *build* are formed by changing the **d** to **t**. The old form of the verb build was *builded* in the past tense. That form is no longer used. The simpler form *built* has taken its place.

An **irregular verb** is a verb that does *not* form the past tense and the past participle in the regular way; that is, by adding **d** or **ed** to the form of the present tense. The past tense and the past participle of irregular verbs are formed in various ways. The most common way is by a change in the vowel; for example, *sing, sang, sung.* In the case of a few verbs, the same form is used for the present tense, the past tense and the past participle: *hurt, hurt, hurt.*

Verb	Past Tense	Past Participle
sing	sang	sung
drive	drove	driven
begin	began	begun
go	went	gone
burst	burst	burst

The past tense and the past participle of the verb *sing* are formed by a change in vowel. The **i** in *sing* changes to **a** in the past tense (*sang*) and to **u** in the past participle (*sung*). The verb *begin* follows a similar change in the vowel. The verb *go* has a different form for the past tense and for the past participle: *go, went, gone.* The verb *burst* has the same form for the present tense, the past tense, and the past participle.

VERBS ADDED TO THE LANGUAGE

New verbs are added to the English language as the need arises. Practically all of new verbs form the past tense and the past participle by adding **ed** or **d**; that is, they follow the pattern of the regular verbs. To form the past tense or the past participle of these verbs add **ed** or **d**.

Verb	Past Tense	Past Participle
activate	activated	activated
radio	radioed	radioed
camouflage	camouflaged	camouflaged
audition	auditioned	auditioned
laminate	laminated	laminated

THE TROUBLESOME VERBS

The *regular verbs* cause very little trouble in speaking and writing because the past tense and the past participle usually follow the rule of forming the past tense and the past participle by adding **d** or **ed.** It is the *irregular verbs* that are responsible for most of the verb errors.

Errors are frequently made in using the *past tense* and the *perfect tense* forms of irregular verbs. This is due to the fact that these verbs form the past tense and the perfect tenses irregularly. In order to use these verbs correctly, it is highly important for you to become familiar with the principal parts of the irregular verbs that are in common use. You will learn these forms by checking constantly until you are familiar with the correct forms for the past tense and the past participle.

Mistakes are commonly made in using the wrong form for the **past tense:** *done* for *did*; *seen* for *saw*; *come* for *came*; *swum* for *swan*; *dove* for *dived*; *run* for *ran*; *drunk* for *drank*. Mistakes are also made in using the wrong form for the **past participle:** *went* for *gone*; *did* for *done*; *swam* for *swum*; *tore* for *torn*; *began* for *begun*; *came* for *come*. The past participle is used in forming the perfect tenses.

Correct Forms for the Past Tense

I <u>did</u> the work assigned to me. (not *done*)

We <u>saw</u> the parade yesterday. (not *seen*)

He <u>came</u> from Ireland two years ago. (not *come*)

She <u>swam</u> across the English Channel last summer. (not *swum*)

The swimming teacher <u>dived</u> off the pier. (not *dove*)
The boy <u>ran</u> through the traffic. (not *run*)
We <u>drank</u> all the milk in the pitcher. (not *drunk*)

Correct Forms for the Past Participle
The delegates **have gone** home. (not *have went*)
He **has done** the work well. (not *has did*)
She **has swum** the channel several times. (not *has swam*)
The actress **has torn** her dress. (not *has tore*)
They **have begun** to check the accounts. (not *have began*)
Has the mail **come**? (not *has came*)

In the first sentence, the past participle is *gone*. It is combined with the auxiliary *have* to form the verb phrase *have gone*. The form *went* should never be used with *have, has* or *had*.

In the second sentence, the past participle is *done*. It is the correct form of the verb to combine with *has*. In the third sentence, the past participle is *swum*. It is correctly used with *has. Tore* should never be used with *have, has*, or *had* The correct form is *have, has*, or *had torn*.

Began is the correct form for the past tense. It should not be used for the past participle. The correct form for the past participle is *begun*. Never use the forms *have began, had began*, or *has began*. The correct forms are *have begun, had begun*, and *has begun*.

The following table gives the principal parts of the irregular verbs that cause most of the verb errors. You should become familiar with the principal parts of these verbs. Consult this list whenever you are in doubt about the correct form to use. If the verb you want is not in this list, consult a reliable, up-to-date dictionary. The principal parts of verbs are given in most dictionaries.

PRINCIPAL PARTS OF TROUBLESOME VERBS

Present Tense (present time)	**Past Tense** (past time)	**Past Participle** (*used with have, has, had*)
awake	awaked	awaked
	awoke	awoke
be (am)	was	been
beat	beat	beaten
become	became	become
begin	began	begun
bid (offer)	bid	bid
bid (Command)	bade	bidden, bid
blow	blew	blown
break	broke	broken
bring	brought	brought
broadcast	broadcast	broadcast
	broadcasted	broadcasted
burst	burst	burst
catch	caught	caught
choose	chose	chosen
climb	climbed	climbed
come	came	come
cut	cut	cut
dive	dived	dived
do	did	done
drag	dragged	dragged
draw	drew	drawn
drink	drank	drunk
drive	drove	driven
drown	drowned	drowned

eat	ate	eaten
fall	fell	fallen
flow	flowed	flowed
fly	flew	flown
forget	forgot	
		forgot
freeze	froze	frozen
get	got	got, gotten
give	gave	given
go	went	gone
hang (a picture)	hung	hung
hang (a criminal)	hanged	hanged
know	knew	known
lay (to place, to put)	laid	laid
lead	led	led
leave	left	left
lend	lent	lent
let	let	let
lie (recline)	lay (not laid)	lain (not laid)
lie (false)	lied	lied
lose	lost	lost
prove	proved	proved
ride	rode	ridden
ring	rang	rung
rise	rose	risen (not rose)
run	ran	run
say	said	said
see	saw	seen
send	sent	sent
set	set	set
shake	shook	shaken

shine (light)	shone	shone
shine (polish)	shined	shined
show	showed	shown, showed
shrink	shrank	shrunk
sing	sang	sung
sink	sank	sunk
sit	sat	sat
spring	sprang, sprung	sprung
steal	stole	stolen
swear	swore	sworn
swim	swam	swum
swing	swung	swung
take	took	taken
teach	taught	taught
tear	tore	torn
tell	told	told
think	thought	thought
throw	threw	thrown
try	tried	tried
understand	understood	understood
wake	waked, woke	waked
wear	wore	worn
weave	wove	woven
weep	wept	wept
wind	wound	wound
wring	wrung	wrung
write	wrote	written

SIX CONFUSING VERBS

Six of the irregular verbs require special attention and study because they are so frequently confused. As a result, they are used incorrectly more often than any of the other irregular verbs. These forms of the verbs in each pair are somewhat similar, but the meanings are quite different. We shall make a special study of these verbs so that you will be able to use them correctly.

LIE AND LAY

There are two different verbs that are spelled alike (*lie*). One means to tell a falsehood. This is a regular verb and causes no difficulty, either in speaking or in writing. The verb that is confused with *lay* is the verb *lie*, which means *to recline, to rest,* or *to remain in a reclining position.* This verb is an irregular verb. The principal parts are *lie, lay,* and (*have, has, had*) *lain.* The present participle, the form that ends in *ing,* is *lying.*

There are two important facts regarding the verb *lie* (to recline) that you should always keep in mind: (1) There is no form ending in **d** that belongs to the verb *lie,* meaning *to recline.* The form *laid* should never be used when you mean *to recline, rest,* or *remain in a reclining position.* (2) The verb *lie* never takes an object.

Mother **lies** down every afternoon. (*rests, reclines*)
Mother **lay** on the couch all afternoon. (not *laid*)
Mother **is lying** on the couch. (not *laying*)
Mother **has lain** on that couch often. (not *has laid*)

The verb *lie* is also the verb to use when we speak about inanimate objects that are in a reclining or in a *lying down* position.

The pen **lies** on my desk. (not *lays*)
The pen **lay** on my desk all day. (not *laid*)
The pen **is lying** on my desk. (not *is laying*)
The pen **has lain** on my desk all week. (not *has laid*)

The verb **lay,** that is so often confused with *lie,* means *to put something down, to place something somewhere.* The prin-

cipal parts of this verb are *lay, laid,* (*have, has,* or had) *laid.*
The present participle is *laying.* The verb *lay* always takes an
object.

John **lays** carpets for Macey's store. (*carpets* object of *lays*)
John **laid** carpets all week. (*carpets* object of *laid*)
John **has laid** carpets for many years. (*carpets* object of *has
laid*)

In the first sentence, the verb *lays* is the present tense of the
verb *lay,* which means to put something down. The word
carpets is the direct object of the verb *lays.* It tells what John
put down. In the second sentence, the verb *laid* is the past
tense of the verb *lay.*

When we use the form *laid,* we must supply an object telling
what we *laid,* or *what we put down. Carpets* is the direct object
of the verb *laid.* It tells what John *laid.* In the last sentence,
laid is the correct form of the verb *lay* to combine with *has.*
It helps form the verb phrase *has laid.*

SIT AND SET

The verb *sit* means to *assume a sitting position* or *to occupy
a seat.* The principal parts of the verb *sit* are *sit, sat,* (*have,
has, had*) *sat.* The present participle is *sitting.* The verb *sit*
never takes an object. The form *set* does not belong to this
verb.

Joe **sat** very still, watching the game.
The children **were sitting** on the floor.
I always **sit** near the fireplace when I read.
My aunt likes **to sit** in a rocking chair.
She **has sat** in the same chair for many years.

The verb *set* means *to place, to put something in position,
to make rigid, solid,* or *stiff.* The principal parts of the verb
set are *set, set,* (*have, has, had*) *set.* The present participle is
setting. The verb *set* usually takes an object. There are a few

idiomatic uses of the verb in which it does *not* take an object. The verb *set* takes an object in the following sentences:

Esther **set** the basket on the table. (*basket* direct object)
We **set** the clock back yesterday. (*clock* direct object)
The operator **set** her hair beautifully. (*hair* direct object)
The buyer **has set** the price too low. (*price* direct object)

Idiomatic Uses

The verb *set* is used *without an object* in the following sentences. Study the types of situations in which the verb *set* is used without an object. These are idiomatic uses of the verb *set*.

The sun **was setting** when we left the lodge.
The cement **will set** in two hours.
We **set** out on a long journey.
The men **set** to work at once.
Jelly **sets** as it cools.

RISE AND RAISE

The verb *rise* means to *ascend, to go up, to extend upward, to swell up,* as bread dough in fermentation, *to increase in value, force* or *intensity.* The principal parts of the verb *rise* are *rise, rose,* and (*have, has, had*) *risen.* The present participle is *rising.* The verb *rise* expresses action, but it does not take an object.

The building **rises** to a height of eighty feet.
This river **rises** in the north.
The tide **was rising.**
Dan **has risen** in his profession.
The plane **rose** steadily.
The sun **will rise** at six o'clock tomorrow.
The cliffs **rise** far above the sea.

The verb *raise* means *to lift up something* or cause it *to go up, to increase the amount or price, to collect a number of things*, etc. The verb *raise* always takes an object. You can't raise without raising something. The verb *raise* is a regular verb. The principal parts are *raise, raised, raised*. The present participle is *raising*.

I **raised** my arm. (to lift up)
Don't **raise** so much dust! (to cause to rise)
The leader **raised** an army. (collected)
We **shall raise** the flag at sunrise. (to cause to go up)
The farmer **raises** wheat. (to cause to grow)
The landlord **raised** the rent. (increased)
Do not **raise** your voice. (to make louder)

13. THE TENSES OF VERBS

THE SIX TENSES

A verb is the most important word in any sentence because more constructions depend upon the verb than upon any other part of speech. Verbs have a number of properties which other parts of speech do not have. One of the properties that belongs exclusively to verbs and verb forms is tense.

Chapter 12 explained that in grammar *tense* means *time*. Verbs have **six tenses** which show differences in the time of *action* or the time of the *state of being* or *condition* (linking verbs).

I *see* a robin on the fence. (**present** time)
I *saw* a robin on the fence yesterday. (**past time**)
I *shall see* a number of birds when I go to the woods. (**future** time)

These sentences do not mean the same thing. The meaning depends to a large extent upon the verb form that is used; that is, the verb form that is used to show the *time* of the action.

The first sentence means that the action expressed by the verb *see* is going on now. The second sentence means that the action expressed by the verb *saw* happened at some time in the past (yesterday). The third sentence means that the action expressed by the verb *shall see* will occur at some future time.

The verbs used in the three sentences are forms of the verb *see*. The verb *see* in the first sentence is the form used in the present tense. It expresses or denotes *present time*. The verb *saw* in the second sentence is the form used to express *past time*. The verb *shall see* is the form used to express *future time*.

Remember, there are six tenses in English. The three tenses which you have just studied are called the **simple tenses.**

The other three tenses are called the **perfect tenses.** The only difference between the simple tenses and the perfect tenses is that the perfect tenses include the idea of completion. In grammar, the word *perfect* refers to an action or state of being that is completed at the time of speaking or writing.

Simple Tenses	**Perfect Tenses**
present tense	*present perfect* tense
past tense	*past perfect* tense
future tense	*future perfect* tense

THE SIMPLE TENSES

The present tense denotes *present time*. It is also used to express *habitual action*, or to express an idea that is *generally accepted as true*.

I *hear* the bell. (present time)
Oscar *works* in an airplane factory. (habitual action)
"Honesty *is* the best policy." (generally accepted truth)

The present tense is often used to express *future time*. Examine the following sentences carefully. In all of them the present tense expresses a future idea:

If it *rains*, we shall not go to the woods.
If the bill *passes*, the tax will be removed.
Our lease on the factory *expires* tomorrow.

The past tense denotes *past time*. The past tense of **regular verbs** is formed by adding *d* or *ed* to the present tense form: call, call*ed*; dive, div*ed*. Sometimes the *d* at the end of the present tense form changes to *t* in the past tense: build, buil*t*.

I *mailed* the letter yesterday. (addition of *ed*)
We *dived* into the pool. (addition of *d*)
The hunter *built* a cabin in the woods. (change of *d* to *t*)

The past tense of **irregular verbs** is formed in various ways. Sometimes there is a change in the vowel: s*i*ng, s*a*ng;

swim, swam; begin, began; drive, drove; break, broke. Sometimes the same form is used in the past tense and in the present tense: bid, bid; hurt, hurt; cut, cut; slit, slit.

The future tense denotes *future time*. The future tense is formed by combining the auxiliary *shall* or *will* with the present tense form of the verb. Use *shall* with the pronouns I and we. Use *will* with the pronouns *you, he, she, it, they.*

I *shall see* you tomorrow. (*shall* first person)
I am sure that you *will be* late. (*will* second person)
The speaker *will arrive* at seven. (*will* third person)

To express future time, use *shall* in the first person and *will* in the second and third persons.

THE PERFECT TENSES

You can remember the *perfect tenses* easily, if you remember that the work **perfect** is always used in identifying them. The three perfect tenses are the *present perfect tense*, the *past perfect tense*, and the *future perfect tense*.

The present perfect tense denotes *action that is completed* at the time of speaking or writing. It may also indicate action that is *continuing into the present*.

The present perfect tense is formed by combining the auxiliary *have* or *has* with the past participle of the principal verb. The auxiliary *has* is always used in the third person singular: He *has spoken* to the manager.

I *have seen* three of Shaw's plays. (*have seen* first person)
You *have earned* a promotion. (*have earned* second person)
John *has washed* the car. (*has washed* third person)

In the first sentence, the verb phrase is *have seen*. It is in the present perfect tense. The verb phrase is made up of the auxiliary *have* and the past participle of the verb *see*, which is *seen* (*have seen*). In the third sentence, the auxiliary *has* is used instead of *have* (*has washed*).

114

The past perfect tense denotes *action that was completed* before some definite time in the past. The past perfect tense is formed by combining the auxiliary *had* with the past participle of the principal verb: *had walked, had known, had given, had drunk, had become, had been*, etc.

In the following sentences, verbs in the past tense are underlined once. Verbs in the past perfect tense are underlined twice.

By the time the officer arrived, the thief had disappeared.

I liked the speaker better after I had heard him the second time.

The agent had sold all the tickets before I applied for mine.

The future perfect tense denotes *action that will be completed* at some definite time in the future. The future perfect tense is seldom used in informal speaking or writing.

The future perfect tense is formed by combining the auxiliaries *shall have* or *will have* with the past participle of the principal verb. *Shall have* is used in the first person, and *will have* in the second and third persons.

The *italicized* words are in the future perfect tense.

My friend *will have sailed* before I reach the pier.

By January, the committee *will have completed* the investigation.

I *shall have crossed* the river three times before noon.

Many verb errors are made because the writer or speaker is not familiar with the forms for the past tense and the past participle. Whenever you are not sure of one of these forms, consult the tables in Chapter 12. If the verb you are interested in is not listed, consult a reliable, up-to-date dictionary. You will find these forms listed after the verb.

You can also avoid verb errors if you know the auxiliaries that indicate the tense:

shall and *will* for the future tense
have and *has* for the present perfect tense
had for the past perfect tense
shall have or *will have* for the future perfect tense

THE VERB "TO BE"

Every person should be thoroughly familiar with the forms of the verb **to be.** It is the most irregular, and also the most important verb in the English language. The verb *to be* is used as an independent verb, and is also used as an auxiliary verb. The entire passive voice and all the progressive forms of other verbs are formed by using the verb *to be* as an auxiliary or helping verb. You should become familiar with the forms for the six tenses of this important verb.

On the following pages you will find reference tables for the tenses of three verbs: the verb *to be*, the regular verb *call*, and the irregular verb *ring*. Study these tables carefully.

SIX TENSES OF THE VERB "TO BE"

Singular and Plural

PRESENT TENSE

First person: I am
                      we are

Second person: you are
                      you are

Third person: he, she, it is
                      they are

PAST TENSE

First person: I was

116

we were

Second person: you were
                          you were

Third person: he, she, it was
                          they were

FUTURE TENSE

First person: I *shall* be
                          we *shall* be

Second person: you *will* be
                          you *will* be

Third person: he, she, it *will* be
                          they *will* be.

PRESENT PERFECT TENSE

First person: I *have* been
                          we *have* been

Second person: you *have* been
                          you *have* been

Third person: he, she, it *has* been
                          they *have* been

PAST PERFECT TENSE

First person: I *had* been
                          we *had* been

Second person: you *had* been
                          you *had* been

Third person: he, she, it *had* been
                          they *had* been

VERB "TO BE" (cont'd)

Singular and Plural

FUTURE PERFECT TENSE

First person:	I *shall have* been we *shall have* been
Second person:	you *will have* been you *will have* been
Third person:	he, she, it *will have* been they *will have* been

THE SIX TENSES OF A REGULAR VERB

VERB "CALL" ACTIVE VOICE

Singular and Plural

PRESENT TENSE

First person:	I call we call
Second person:	you call you call
Third person:	he, she, it *calls* they call

PAST TENSE

First person:	I call*ed* we call*ed*
Second person:	you call*ed* you call*ed*
Third person:	he, she, it call*ed* they call*ed*

FUTURE TENSE

First person: I *shall* call
we *shall* call

Second person: you *will* call
you *will* call

Third person: he, she, it *will* call
they *will* call

PRESENT PERFECT TENSE

First person: I *have* called
we *have* called

Second person: you *have* called
you *have* called

Third person: he, she, it *has* called
they *have* called

PAST PERFECT TENSE

First person: I *had* called
we *had* called

Second person: you *had* called
you *had* called

Third person: he, she, it *had* called
they *had* called

FUTURE PERFECT TENSE

First person: I *shall have* called
we *shall have* called

Second person: you *will have* called
you *will have* called

Third person: he, she, it *will have* called
they *will have* called

SIX TENSES OF AN IRREGULAR VERB

VERB "RING" ACTIVE VOICE
Singular and Plural

PRESENT TENSE

First person:	I ring
	we ring
Second person:	you ring
	you ring
Third person:	he, she, it *rings*
	they ring

PAST TENSE

First person:	I rang
	we rang
Second person:	you rang
	you rang
Third person:	he, she, it rang
	they rang

FUTURE TENSE

First person:	I *shall* ring
	we *shall* ring
Second person:	you *will* ring
	you *will* ring
Third person:	he, she, it *will* ring
	they *will* ring

PRESENT PERFECT TENSE

First person:	I have rung

	we have rung
Second person:	you have rung
	you have rung
Third person:	he, she, it has rung
	they have rung

PAST PERFECT TENSE

First person:	I had rung
	we had rung
Second person:	you had rung
	you had rung
Third person:	he, she, it had rung
	they had rung

FUTURE PERFECT TENSE

First person:	I shall have rung
	we shall have rung
Second person:	you will have rung
	you will have rung
Third person:	he, she, it will have rung
	they will have rung

PROGRESSIVE FORMS OF VERBS

In addition to the forms which have already been given to show tense, a verb has special forms to show that the *action is continuing*. These forms are called the **progressive forms** of a verb. The *progressive forms* are used to show that an action is *continuing* or *progressing* at the time indicated by a particular tense.

I *am studying* English. (The action is continuing.)
He *is planning* a trip to Mexico. (The action is continuing.)

The progressive form of a verb is made up by using some form of the verb *to be* with the *ing* form of the principal verb.

The form of a verb that ends in *ing* is called the **present participle.**

In the first sentence, the progressive form of the verb is *am studying*. It is made up of a form of the verb *to be*, which is *am*, and the present participle of the principal verb, which is *studying*. In the second sentence, the progressive form of the verb, *is planning*, is made up in a similar way.

The following are the progressive forms of the verb *call* for the six tenses (first person, singular).

I *am calling* you. (present progressive)
I *was calling* you. (past progressive)
I *shall be calling* you. (future progressive)
I *have been calling* you. (present perfect progressive)
I *had been calling* you. (past perfect progressive)
I *shall have been calling* you. (future perfect progressive)

The present tense, progressive form often expresses a future idea. The verb *to go* is commonly used in this way:

I *am going* to New York next week. (in the future)
He *is going* to buy a new home in the suburbs. (in the future)

VERB "CALL"

PROGRESSIVE FORMS ACTIVE VOICE

PRESENT TENSE

First Person: I *am* calling
we *are* calling

Second person: you *are* calling
you *are* calling

Third person: he, she, it *is* calling
they *are* calling

PAST TENSE

First person: I *was* calling
we *were* calling

Second person: you *were* calling
you *were* calling

Third person: he, she, it *was* calling
they *were* calling

FUTURE TENSE

First person: I *shall be* calling
we *shall be* calling

Second person: you *will be* calling
you *will be* calling

Third person: he, she, it *will be* calling
they *will be* calling

PRESENT PERFECT TENSE

First person: I *have been* calling
we *have been* calling

Second person: you *have been* calling

PROGRESSIVE FORMS ACTIVE VOICE

PRESENT PERFECT TENSE

	you have been calling
Third person:	he, she, it *has been* calling
	they *have been* calling

PAST PERFECT TENSE

First person:	I *had been* calling
	we *had been* calling
Second person:	you *had been* calling
	you *had been* calling
Third person:	he, she, it *had been* calling
	they *had been* calling

FUTURE PERFECT TENSE

First person:	I *shall have been* calling
	we *shall have been* calling
Second person:	you *will have been* calling
	you *will have been* calling
Third person:	he, she, it *will have been* calling
	they *will have been* calling

EMPHATIC FORMS OF THE VERB

The **emphatic forms** of a verb are often used to give greater emphasis to the idea expressed by the verb. The auxiliaries *do, does,* and *did* are used to give this additional emphasis. The emphatic forms are used in only two tenses, the *present tense* and the *past tense*.

I *do agree* with you. (present tense)
Jane *did send* the letter. (past tense)

The editor *does need* to know the facts. (present tense)

EMPHATIC FORMS — *PRESENT TENSE*

Singular and Plural

First person:	I *do* call
	we *do* call
Second person:	you *do* call
	you *do* call
Third person:	he *does* call
	they *do* call

EMPHATIC FORMS—*PAST TENSE*

First person:	I *did* call
	we *did* call
Second person:	you *did* call
	you *did* call
Third person:	he *did* call
	they *did* call

When *do*, *does*, and *did* are used in questions, the form is not used for emphasis. The use of *do*, *does*, and *did* in questions is an idiomatic way of asking question in English. In the following questions *do*, *does*, and *did* are not the emphatic form of the verb:

Did he buy that hat last week?
Do you know her?
Does he want to pay the bill?

Also, when *do*, *does*, and *did* are used to mean *accomplish, carry out*, etc., the form is not used for emphasis in these cases. This sentence is an example:

We *did* our homework quickly.

125

THE USE OF SHALL AND WILL

Many of the precise distinctions concerning the use of *shall* and *will* are rapidly passing out of informal speaking and writing. Careful writers, however, still observe some of these distinctions. The following are some of the distinctions that are most generally observed:

Simple Futurity

Use *shall* in the first person and *will* in the second and third persons to express **simple futurity.** Simple futurity means anticipation or expectation of what is likely to happen, or what one is likely to do. It follows the regular forms of the future tense:

First person:	I *shall* go
	we *shall* go
Second person:	you *will* go
	you *will* go
Third person:	he *will* go
	they *will* go

Determination, Threat, Promise

If you want to express determination, compulsion, threat, or promise (willingness to do something), reverse the order of *shall* and *will*. Use *will* in the first person, and *shall* in the second and third persons.

First person:	I *will* go
	we *will* go
Second person:	you *shall* go
	you *shall* go
Third person:	he *shall* go
	they *shall* go

Special Cases

When *shall* and *will* are followed by such expressions as *be glad, be sorry, be happy, be delighted, be pleased*, etc., use *shall* in the first person, and *will* in the second and third persons. If *will* is used in the first person, it would mean that you are determined *to be glad, sorry, delighted*, etc. If *shall* is used in the second and third persons, it would mean that you are compelling someone *to be glad, sorry*, etc. The following are the accepted ways of using such expressions:

I shall be glad to see you. (not *will*)
We shall be delighted to help you. (not *will*)
You will be sorry to learn of his misfortune. (not *shall*)
He will be pleased to see you at four. (not *shall*)

In giving courteous commands, you should use *will* in the second and third persons instead of *shall*. This is the form that is generally followed in giving military orders and instructions:

Corporal Smith *will report* to Captain Allen. (not *shall report*)
You *will hand* in your report on Wednesday. (not *shall*)
The meeting *will come* to order. (not *shall*)
Mr. Ames, you *will meet* with the committee today. (not *shall*)

SHOULD AND WOULD

Should is the past tense of *shall* and in general, follows the same rules that apply to the use of *shall*. *Would* is the past tense of *will* and follows the same rules that apply to the use of *will*.

Both *should* and *would* have special uses. *Would* is used in all three persons to express *habitual* or *customary* action. *Should* is often used in all three persons to express *obligation*. *Ought* and *should* both express obligation and are used interchangeable.

Every evening we *would play* cards for hours. (*habitual action*)

127

You *should read* something worth while every day. (*obligation*)

You *ought to read* something worth while every day. (*obligation*)

Study the following sentences carefully. Note especially the explanations given in parentheses. This will help you understand the distinctions which have been made in the preceding discussion:

I shall go to the theater this evening. (*simple futurity—expectation*)

I will not *see* him today. (*determination* on the part of the speaker)

You will enjoy meeting him. (*simple futurity* or *expectation*)

He will enter Harvard in September. (*simple futurity*)

I will accompany you to the clinic. (*promise—willingness*)

He shall report to the judge every month. (*I am determined* that he shall.)

You shall have any assistance that you may need. (*I am determined* that you shall.)

We shall be pleased to grant you an interview. (*simple futurity*)

You would drown if you ventured out in deep water. (*simple futurity*)

He would drown if he ventured out in deep water. (*simple futurity*)

We should be very happy if *you would call* for us. (*simple futurity*)

I should be the first one to volunteer. (*obligation*)

You should read good books. (*obligation*)

They should offer their services to the committee. (*obligation*)

MIXED TENSES

Unless there is a good reason for making a change, the tenses of the verbs in a sentence or in a paragraph should agree. If you start out with a verb in the *past tense*, you should not change to another verb in the *present tense*. If you start with a verb in the *present tense*, you should not change to the *past tense*.

Tense means *time*, and when you change the tense, you also change the time. Tenses must be consistent; that is, there must be a logical sequence of time. It is illogical to shift from one tense to another tense. Study the following illustrations carefully:

Dr. Smith *examined* the patient and *calls* the nurse. (*incorrect*)

In this sentence, the verb *examined* is in the past tense. It is followed by the verb *calls* which is in the present tense. There is a shift from the past tense to the present tense. Both verbs should be in the past tense or both verbs should be in the present tense.

Dr. Smith *examines* the patient and *calls* the nurse. (*correct*)
or
Dr. Smith *examined* the patient and *called* the nurse. (*correct*)

I *went* into the hall and there I *see* a strange man. (*incorrect*)
I *went* into the hall and there I saw a strange man. (*correct*)

The officer *stopped* the car and *speaks* to the driver. (*incorrect*)
The officer *stopped* the car and *spoke* to the driver. (*correct*)

THE "OF" ERROR

Careless speakers and writers often use the preposition *of* in place of the auxiliary verb *have*. The word *of* is a preposition and should never be used as part of a verb phrase.

The "*of*" error is generally caused by the use of contractions or by careless enunciation on the part of a speaker. The mistake is commonly made after the words *could, might, ought to, should,* and *would*. When *have* is used following any of these words, and the two words are contracted, the resulting combination sounds as if *of* were being used rather than *have:* *could've* sounds like *could of, should've* sounds like *should of*, etc.

Since in speech the contracted form of *have* cannot readily be distinguished from *of*, many persons have the mistaken belief that *of* is the word being said and that it is the correct word to use. As a result they carry over the mistake from their speech into their writing, and never know they are in error. To avoid making the "*of*" error when you are speaking, never contract *have* to *'ve*.

Study the following examples. The presposition *of* should never be used in place of *have* as part of a verb phrase.

We should *of* been more careful. (*incorrect*)
We should *have* been more careful. (*correct*)

He must *of* taken it. (*incorrect*)
He must *have* taken it. (*correct*)

They might *of* notified us. (*incorrect*)
They might *have* notified us. (*correct*)

I should *of* prepared the report. (*incorrect*)
I should *have* prepared the report. (*correct*)

14. VERBS: VOICE AND MOOD

ACTIVE AND PASSIVE VOICE

A verb not only undergoes certain changes to show *tense*, or the time of the action, but it changes in form to show *voice*. **Voice** is a grammatical term which is used to *tell whether the subject of the séntence is acting or is receiving the action expressed by the verb*.

When the subject is acting, we say that the subject is the *doer*. When the subject is receiving the action, we say that the subject is the *receiver*. If you keep these two terms, *doer* and *receiver*, in mind, you will have no difficulty in understanding what *voice* means in grammar.

Study the following sentences carefully. Note the changes that occur in the form of the verb. Note the change that occurs in the subject of the sentence:

<u>Ned washed</u> the car. (*Ned* is the *doer* of the action.)

<u>The car was washed</u> by Ned. (*Car* is the·*receiver* of the action.)

In the first sentence, the subject is *Ned*. He is the *doer*, the one who is performing the action expressed by the verb *washed*. The *car* is receiving the action. In grammar we say that the verb in this sentence is in the **active voice** because the subject is the *doer*, or is doing the washing. The car is the *receiver* of the action.

The second sentence is written in the reverse order. The subject is now the receiver of the action instead of the doer. In order to express this idea, it was necessary to use another verb form, *was washed*. What happened to *Ned*, the doer? *Ned* is still in the sentence but is now in a phrase introduced by the preposition *by*.

The verb *was washed* is in the **passive voice** because it represents the subject of the sentence as the receiver of the action. In other words, the subject is not acting, but is *passive*.

131

The doer, or the actor, appears in a phrase introduced by the preposition *by*.

A verb in the passive voice is *never* a simple verb. It is always a verb phrase. In the sentence, *Our car was stolen yesterday*, the verb *was stolen* is in the *passive voice*. The subject is the receiver of the action. Since the doer is unknown, the "by phrase" is omitted. But we know that it was stolen by someone. If we discover who stole the car, the doer might be added to the sentence:

Our car was stolen yesterday by two strangers.

If a verb is in the **active voice**, *the subject is the doer of the action*. If a verb is in the **passive voice**, *the subject is the receiver of the action*. When a verb is in the passive voice, the doer is often omitted. Sometimes the doer is unknown, and sometimes the doer is so evident that it is not necessary to include the "*by* phrase.'

HOW THE PASSIVE VOICE IS FORMED

You cannot express an idea in the passive voice without using an auxiliary or helping verb. The verb *to be* is the auxiliary verb that is used to help form the six tenses of the passive voice. If you are familiar with the conjugation of the verb *to be*, you will have no difficulty in forming the passive voice of any verb that takes an object.

The passive voice is formed by combining the verb *to be* with the **past participle** of the principal verb. The principal verb is the verb that names the action.

The verb *was washed* in the sentence, *The car was washed by Ned*, is made up of the auxiliary verb *was*, which is a form of the verb *to be*. The *past participle* of the principal verb is added to the auxiliary *was*. The past participle of the verb *wash* is *washed*. The verb phrase is *was washed*. It is a verb phrase in the passive voice.

The verb phrases in the following sentences are in the *passive voice*. They are formed by combining some form of the verb *to be* with the past participle of the principal verb, or the verb that names the action.

The plans will be made by the general.

Trees have been planted in the park by the commissioners.

The verb in the first sentence is *will be made*. It is made up of the auxiliary *will be*, which is a form of the verb *to be* and the past participle of the verb *make*, which is *made*.

The verb in the second sentence is *have been planted*. It is made up of the auxiliary verb *have been*, which is a form of the verb *to be* and the past participle of the verb *plant* (*planted*).

The six tenses of the verb *call* were given in Chapter Thirteen for the *active voice*. The forms for the *passive voice* follow. If you examine these forms carefully, you will see that the tenses follow the regular conjugation of the verb *to be*. The past participle of the verb *call* (*called*) is added to the forms of the verb *to be*.

SIX TENSES OF THE VERB "CALL"

PASSIVE VOICE
Singular and Plural

PRESENT TENSE

First person:	I *am* called
	we are called
Second person:	you *are* called
	you *are* called
Third person:	he *is* called
	they *are* called

VERB "CALL" (cont'd)

PASSIVE VOICE
Singular and Plural

PAST TENSE

First person:
I *was* called
we *were* called

Second person:
you *were* called
you *were* called

Third person:
he *was* called
they *were* called

FUTURE TENSE

First person:
I *shall be* called
we *shall be* called

Second person:
you *will be* called
you *will be* called

Third person:
he *will be* called
they *will be* called

PRESENT PERFECT TENSE

First person:
I *have been* called
we *have been* called

Second person:
you *have been* called
you *have been* called

Third person:
he *has been* called
they *have been* called

PAST PERFECT TENSE

First person:
I *had been* called
we *had been* called

Second person:
you *had been* called

Third person:	you *had been* called
	he *had been* called
	they *had been* called

FUTURE PERFECT TENSE

First person:	I *shall have been* called
	we *shall have been* called
Second person:	you *will have been* called
	you *will have been* called
Third person:	he *will have been* called
	they *will have been* called

SIX TENSES OF THE IRREGULAR VERB "KNOW"

PASSIVE VOICE
Singular and Plural

PRESENT TENSE

First person:	I *am* known
	we *are* known
Second person:	you *are* known
	you *are* known
Third person:	he *is* known
	they *are* known

PAST TENSE

First person:	I *was* known
	we *were* known
Second person:	you *were* known
	you *were* known
Third person:	he *was* known
	they *were* known

VERB "KNOW" (cont'd)

PASSIVE VOICE
Singular and Plural

FUTURE TENSE

First person:
I *shall be* known
we *shall be* known

Second person:
you *will be* known
you *will be* known

Third person:
he *will be* known
they *will be* known

PRESENT PERFECT TENSE

First person:
I *have been* known
we *have been* known

Second person:
you *have been* known
you *have been* known

Third person:
he *has been* known
they *have been* known

PAST PERFECT TENSE

First person:
I *had been* known
we *had been* known

Second person:
you *had been* known
you *had been* known

Third person:
he *had been* known
they *had been* known

FUTURE PERFECT TENSE

First person:
I *shall have been* known
we *shall have been* known

Second person:
you *will have been* known

Third person:

you *will have been* known
he *will have been* known
they *will have been* known

WHEN TO USE THE PASSIVE VOICE

Since you may show that the subject is either the doer or the receiver of the action, the question naturally arises, "Which form is better?" The use of the passive voice often results in a roundabout, awkward method of expression.

In the large majority of cases the *active voice is the better form to use.* Never use the passive voice, either in speaking or writing, when the active voice would be more natural or more direct. The following illustrations show clearly that the active voice would be more natural and more direct than the passive voice.

The concert was enjoyed by us. (*passive voice*)
We enjoyed the concert. (*active voice*)

Your order was sent by us by express today. (*passive voice*)
We sent your order by express today. (*active voice*)

The stranger was barked at by a dog. (*passive voice*)
A dog barked at the stranger. (*active voice*)

As a rule, the active voice is preferred for business writing, and for any other form of writing that requires the direct approach. The use of the *active voice increases vividness.* The passive voice expresses reversed action, since the receiver comes before the doer. Active verbs are often used in newspapers headlines because they are more vivid and take less space. The following headlines are all in the active voice:

"Lion Gets Out of Cage"
"White Sox Capture First Title"
"Urges France to Begin Defense Plan"

137

"Governor Advises Aid for Workers"

The passive voice is generally used when the subject of the sentence is *indefinite, general,* or *unimportant*. In the sentence, *They mine coal in Pennsylvania,* the subject is so indefinite that it is not clear what is meant by *they*. It might mean the miners, the people, or the companies. This sentence, and sentences like it, are improved by putting the verb in the passive voice.

They *mine* coal in Pennsylvania. (*poor*)
Coal *is mined* in Pennsylvania. (*better*)

They *grow* wheat in many of our states. (*poor*)
Wheat *is grown* in many of our states. (*better*)

They *use* tractors on most farms. (*poor*)
Tractors *are used* on most farms. (*better*)

The passive voice is also used when *what was done* is more important than the doer of the action. Study the following sentences:

The play, "Man and Superman," *was written* by Shaw. (*passive*)
Shaw *wrote* the play "Man and Superman." (*active*)

America *was discovered* by Columbus. (*passive*)
Columbus *discovered* America. (*active*)

In the first sentence, if you wish to emphasize the play more than the author, put the verb in the passive voice. In the third sentence, if you wish to emphasize the discovery more than the discoverer, put the verb in the passive voice.

The use of the passive voice is generally used when you want to emphasize the *receiver* rather than the *doer*. However, in the great majority of cases the active voice is more effective than the passive voice.

MOOD OF VERBS

In addition to tense and voice, verbs have another property which is called mood (or *mode*). The word *mood* comes from a Latin word which means *manner*. When we apply the term mood to verbs, we mean *the manner in which the verb expresses the action or state of being*.

There are three moods in English, the *indicative mood*, the *imperative mood*, and the *subjunctive mood*. The *indicative mood* is used *to make statements* and *to ask questions*. Most of the verbs that you commonly use are in the indicative mood.

The stenographer *wrote* the letter. *(statement of fact)*
Did you hear the President's address? *(question)*

The imperative mood is used to *express a command* or *a request*. The imperative mood is found only in the present tense, second person. The subject is always the pronoun *you*, which is seldom expressed.

Come here at once! *(command)*
Close the door, Jane. *(request)*

The subjunctive mood is used to *express a wish* or *a condition which is contrary to fact*. By contrary to fact we mean something which is not true. A contrary to fact condition is usually introduced by the word *if* or *as if*.

If *he were* here, I would give him the keys. *(He is not here.)*
I wish *I were* in Florida. *(expresses a wish)*

The indicative and the imperative moods do not present any problems in English. The verb has the same form to express a statement or to ask a question. You can identify the imperative mood easily because the subject is *you*, which is usually understood. The imperative mood always expresses a command or a request.

Although most of the forms for the subjunctive have disappeared from our language, there are a few forms left that you should be able to recognize and to use. The verb *to be* still retains more of the subjunctive forms than any other verb. In the following, the subjunctive forms of the verb *to be* are given.

SUBJUNCTIVE FORMS OF VERB "TO BE"

PRESENT TENSE——SINGULAR AND PLURAL

First person:	(If) I *be*
	(If) we *be*
Second person:	(If) you *be*
	(If) you *be*
Third person:	(If) he *be*
	(If) they *be*

PAST TENSE——SINGULAR

First person:	(If) I *were*
Second person:	(If) you *were*
Third person:	(If) he *were*

PRESENT PERFECT TENSE——SINGULAR

First person:	(If) I *have* been
Second person:	(If) you *have* been
Third person:	(If) he *have* been

The subjunctive with *be* (present tense) is almost never used in informal speaking and writing. The subjunctive form *have been* instead of *has been* is also passing out of use.

In the preceding table, the forms for the subjunctive that are different from the indicative are in *italics*; that is, *be* in the present tense; *were* in the past tense, first person, singular, and third person, singular; *have* in the present tense, third person, singular.

There is only one change that occurs in the subjunctive in the case of other verbs. In the present tense, third person, singular, the *s* is dropped in the subjunctive.

The verb *have* has only one form in the subjunctive that is different from the indicative. In the present tense, third person, singular.

If he *have* the time, he will meet with you. (subjunctive)
He *has* the time, he will meet with you. (indicative)

If he fail——— (not *fails*)
If he have——— (not *has*)
If he call——— (not *calls*

The word *if* is not a part of the subjunctive. The forms for the subjunctive are usually given with the word *if* because the group of words in which the subjunctive is used is very frequently introduced by the word *if*.

Although the subjunctive mood is rapidly passing out of use in informal speaking and writing, there are certain uses that are still observed by discriminating writers and speakers. The subjunctive expressing a *wish* and the subjunctive in a *contrary to fact condition* are two of these uses.

USES OF THE SUBJUNCTIVE MOOD

You have just learned that careful writers and speakers use the subjunctive to express a wish, a condition that is contrary to fact (not true), and a condition of uncertainty (it may be true or not true). Sometimes careful writers and speakers also use the subjunctive *in making a suggestion, in making a demand,* or *in expressing a need.*

I wish I *were* a millionaire. (wish)
If I *were* you, I should give up the contest. (contrary to fact)
If this plan *fail,* we shall give up the project. (condition of uncertainty)
I suggest that he *work* full time in the future. (suggestion)
The supervisor insists that the bookkeeper *prove* his report. (a demand)
It is imperative that the play *begin* at once. (a necessity)

141

The subjunctive is used in certain parliamentary expressions, such as the following:

I move that the nominations *be closed*.
He moved that the report of the committee *be accepted*.
She moved that the minutes *be adopted* as read.
I move that the meeting *be adjourned*.

The *two most important* uses of the subjunctive are the subjunctive expressing a wish and the subjunctive in a contrary to fact condition after *if*, *as if*, and *as though*.

15. AGREEMENT OF SUBJECT AND VERB

One of the common errors made both in speaking and writing is the lack of agreement between the subject noun or pronoun and the predicate verb. In order to have harmonious relations between the parts of the sentence, you must have this agreement.

AGREEMENT IN PERSON AND NUMBER

The grammatical principle upon which agreement of subject and verb depends is very simple: *The verb must agree with its subject in person and number*. If the subject of the sentence is singular, the verb must also be in the singular. If the subject is plural, the verb must also be plural. If the subject is in the first person, the verb must also be in the first person. If the subject is in the second or third persons, the verb must agree.

He *doesn't* know the answer. (correct—subject and verb are in third person)
He don't know the answer. (incorrect—lack of agreement)
You were invited to the meeting. (correct—subject and verb are in second person)
You was invited to the meeting. (incorrect—lack of agreement)

In the first sentence the subject and verb agree. The subject *He* is in the third person, singular. The verb *doesn't* is also in the third person, singular. In the second sentence, *He don't* is incorrect. The incorrect form for third person, singular is *doesn't* not *don't*.

Although the rule is very simple, there are a number of problems involved in agreement of subject and verb. These problems are responsible for the errors that are commonly made. Sometimes the speaker or writer does not know whether the subject should be regarded as singular or plural. Sometimes he is not sure about the form of the verb for the singular and for the plural. Sometimes he does not know which word is the real subject of the sentence.

In this unit you will consider some of the problems that are responsible for the errors that occur in making the subject and the verb agree. Your first problem will be the one that occurs when you have a sentence with a compound subject.

AGREEMENT OF VERB WITH COMPOUND SUBJECT

The parts of a compound subject are usually connected by *and, or, nor, either or*, and *neither nor*. Usually, when two or more subjects are connected by *and*, the subject is plural and requires a plural verb. The following examples have compound subjects:

Mary and Jane are taking Spanish.
The *president and the vice-president* speak at every meeting.

In the first sentence, the two parts of the compound subject are connected by *and*. The subject is plural and takes a plural verb, *are*. In the second sentence, the two parts of the compound subject are also connected by *and*. The subject takes the plural form of the verb which is *speak*.

There is one exception to the "and" rule. Sometimes the two subjects connected by *and* form a unit. In this case, *the subject is regarded as singular and takes a singular verb.*

Bacon and eggs is a popular combination. (*Verb is singular.*)
The Stars and Stripes flies overhead. (*Verb is singular.*)

When two subjects connected by *and* refer to the same person or thing, the subject is *singular*.

His companion and friend is very devoted to him. (*same person*)

144

The secretary and treasurer was present at the meeting. (*same person*)

If the subjects in the preceding sentences referred to *two individuals*, the verbs would be plural. The sentences would read as follows:

His companion and his friend are very devoted to him.
The secretary and the treasurer were present at the meeting.

By placing the word *his* before friend and the word *the* before treasurer, you clearly indicate that there are two individuals.

Subjects Connected by "Or" or "Nor"

When two singular subjects are connected by the word *or*, the subject is singular. The sentence means *either the one or the other*. It does not mean *both*. The same rule applies when *nor* is used to join two singular subjects. sed oEither or and *neither nor* follow the same rule.

Mary or Jane is going to the fashion show. (*the one or the other*)
Neither the man nor the boy was responsible. (*neither the one nor the other*)

When one of the subjects connected by *or, nor, either or, neither nor* is singular and the other is plural, the verb agrees with the subject that is *nearer to* it. If both subjects are plural, the verb is also plural.

Neither the boy nor the men were responsible. (*Verb is plural.*)
Neither the men nor the boy was responsible. (*Verb is singular.*)
Neither the men nor the boys were responsible. (*Verb is plural.*)

In the first sentence, the plural subject is nearer to the verb. In the second sentence, the singular subject is nearer to the verb. In the third sentence, both subjects are plural. When one of the subjects is singular and the other is plural, you should put the plural subject nearer to the verb. It makes the verb plural and sounds better.

Either I or they are responsible for the small attendance.

This sentence would sound better if it were written as follows:

Either I am responsible for the small attendance, or they are.

AGREEMENT OF VERB WITH COLLECTIVE NOUNS

A **collective noun** is a noun that represents a group or a collection of objects usually considered as a unit. Words like *crowd, troop, herd, people, flock*, and *jury* are collective nouns.

A collective noun that is singular in meaning requires a singular verb. A collective noun that is plural in meaning requires a plural verb.

If the collective noun in a particular sentence represents the individuals acting as a unit, the noun is singular. If the sentence indicates clearly that the individuals are acting separately, the noun is plural. The following examples will help you see this distinction:

The *committee is opposed* to the plan. (*acting as a unit*)
The *board of directors is* in session. (*as a unit*)
The *jury returned its* verdict. (*as a unit*)
The *jury have returned* to their homes. (*as individuals*)
The *family have given* their contributions. (*as individuals*)

In most cases where the individuals composing a group are acting separately, it is better to use such expressions as *the members of the jury, the members of the family*, etc. These expressions sound better and clearly indicate that the individuals are acting separately.

The members of the jury have returned to their homes.
The people in the audience were waving their hands.

146

INTERVENING PHRASES

Sometimes the subject is followed by prepositional phrases or such expressions as *accompanied by, in accordance with, together with, as well as, including,* etc. The subject of the sentence is not affected in any way by the introduction of such phrases. You will never find the subject of the sentence in a prepositional phrase or in any one of the expressions listed in the following sentences:

A *package* (of books) *was delivered* today.
Materials (for the building) *have been shipped.*
Important *papers,* as well as his will, *were found* in his desk.
The *checks,* including a statement, *were mailed* today.

In the first sentence, the subject is the word *package.* Since package is singular, the verb must be singular. In the second sentence, the subject is the word *Materials.* Since the subject is plural, the verb must be plural. The prepositional phrases, of *books,* and *for the building,* do not affect the number of the subject.

The subject of the third sentence is *papers,* which is plural. The verb must also be plural to agree with the subject. The group of words, *as well as his will,* does not affect the number of the subject. In the fourth sentence, the expression, *including a statement,* does not affect the number of the subject. The subject is *checks,* which is plural. The verb must also be plural, to agree with the subject.

AGREEMENT OF SUBJECT WITH CONTRACTIONS

Contractions are verbs that have been shortened by the omission of one or more letters. The omission of the letters is indicated by the use of an apostrophe. Many persons make mistakes in agreement of subject and verb when they use contractions. The use of the contractions *don't* and *ain't* are responsible for a great many of these errors.

Although the word *ain't* is frequently heard in informal conversation, most educated persons consider its use incorrect and unacceptable.

Do not use *ain't* for *am not, are not,* or *isn't.* The contraction *aren't* should be used for *are not.* There is no contraction for the words *am not.*

I *am not* interested in the position. (not *ain't*)
We *are not* going to the theater. (not *ain't*)
We *aren't* going to the meeting. (not *ain't*)
Isn't this a beautiful day! (not *ain't*)

Another error commonly made is the use of **don't** for **doesn't. Don't** is a contraction for *do not.* It should not be used in the third person, singular. The expressions, *it don't, he don't* and *she don't* are incorrect. Do no misuse them for *it doesn't, he doesn't,* and *she doesn't.*

It *don't* make any difference. (incorrect)
It *doesn't* make any difference. (correct)

He *don't* belong to our union. (incorrect)
He *doesn't* belong to our union. (correct)

AGREEMENT OF VERB WITH INDEFINITE PRONOUNS

The indefinite pronouns *one, no one, anyone, everyone, someone, anybody, nobody, everybody, somebody, each, either,* and *neither* are always singular. Since these pronouns are singular, they take a singular verb.

Only *one* of the candidates is eligible. (*singular verb*)
Each of these bags has been examined. (*singular verb*)
Neither has lost his ticket. (*singular verb*)
Somebody is responsible for the accident. (*singular verb*)

148

Anyone has the right to offer criticism. (*singular verb*)
Nobody has access to the vault. (*singular verb*)

When *many a*, *each*, and *every* are used to introduce a sentence and function as adjectives, the *subject* is singular.

Many a *man* wishes that he had gone to college.
Each *window* and *door* was locked securely.
Every *man*, *woman*, and *child* is expected to report.

The indefinite pronouns *several, few, both* and *many* are always plural.

Several were called to the platform. (*plural verb*)
A *few* were opposed to the bill. (*plural verb*)
Both were anxious to receive the award. (*plural verb*)
Many in the audience objected to his speech. (*plural verb*)

The indefinite pronouns *some, none, any*, and *all* are singular or plural according to the meaning of the sentence. When these words refer to a *quantity* or a *mass* taken as a whole, they are generally considered as singular. When they refer to a *number*, they are regarded as plural in meaning.

Some are going by plane. (*more than one*—plural)
Some of the ice cream *is* left. (*mass or quantity*—singular)
Are any of the men going by plane? (*more than one*—plural)
Is there *any* gasoline in the tank? (*mass or quantity*—singular)
None of these apples *are* ripe. (*more than one*—plural)
We needed a ball but *none was* available. (*not one*—singular)
All of the gasoline *has been sold*. (*mass or quantity*—singular)
All of the women *have brought* gifts. (*more than one*—plural)

Some nouns are plural in form, but singular in meaning. Examples of nouns that take a singular verb are *mumps, measles, news, summons, physics, mathematics*.

Physics is a very interesting subject. *Verb is singular*.)

The news this week is startling. (*Verb is singular*.)
Measles is a contagious disease. (*Verb is singular*.)
Mathematics was his favorite study. (*Verb is singular*.)

SPECIAL CASES OF AGREEMENT

1. Words like *pants, trousers, pliers, scissors, shears,* and *tongs* are plural and take a plural verb. When the word *pair* is used as the subject, the subject is regarded as singular and takes a singular verb.

The *scissors* are very sharp. (*plural*)
A *pair* of scissors was left on the desk. (*singular*)

2. A plural noun which shows *weight, extent,* or *quantity* is singular, and takes a singular verb.

Ten miles is a long distance to walk. (*singular*)
Five dollars is the price of the hat. (*singular*)
Twelve inches is the proper length. (*singular*)

3. The words *half* and *part* are singular or plural according to the meaning of the sentence. When these words refer to a *mass* or a *section*, they are singular. When they refer to a *number* of individuals or things, they are plural.

Half of the boys are in camp. (*number*—plural)
Half of the pie is left. (*mass* or *section*—singular)
Part of the roof was destroyed. (*mass* or *section*—singular)
Part of the guests have arrived. (*number*—plural)

4. When the word *number* is preceded by the article *a*, it takes a plural verb. When it is immediately preceded by the article *the*, it takes a singular verb.

A *number* of men *were working* on the project. (*plural*)
The number of men present *was* small. (*singular*)

5. The name of a firm is often regarded as singular even when there is a plural form in the title. If the entire name carries a plural idea, the name is regarded as plural.

Harrison Brothers are having a sale on furs. (*plural*)

The Lexicon Company publishes books. (*singular*)

General Motors Company has declared a dividend. (*singular*)

6. Sometimes a sentence begins with the word *there* or *here*. Neither of these words could be the subject of the sentence. The word *there* is used either as an expletive or as an adverb. The word *here* is an adverb. When a sentence begins with *here* or *there*, you should transpose it so that the true subject will appear at the beginning of the sentence. Then it will be possible for you to determine whether the subject is singular or plural.

There are six men on the committee.

Six men are on the committee. (*plural subject—plural verb*)

Here comes the general with his staff.

The general comes here with his staff. (*singular subject and verb*)

Sometimes a sentence beginning with the introductory *there* or *here* has a *compound subject*, which requires a plural verb. Mistakes in the number of the verb are frequently made because the speaker or the writer does not realize that the subject is *compound*. When the sentence is transposed, it is easy to determine whether the subject is simple or compound. The following sentences have compound subjects:

There goes the boy and his mother. (incorrect)

There go the boy and his mother. (correct)

The boy and his mother go there. (*compound subject—plural verb*)

Here comes John and Mary. (incorrect)

Here come John and Mary. (correct)

John and Mary come here. (*compound subject—plural verb*)

151

16. PREPOSITIONAL PHRASES

Chapter Two explained that a preposition is a word that shows the relation between its object and some other word in the sentence. In this unit you will study the function of the phrase which the preposition introduces.

A *prepositional phrase consists of the preposition and its object.* Sometimes the noun which serves as the object of the preposition has modifiers, but the important words in the phrase are the two words the *preposition* and the *object.* The prepositions and their objects are underlined.

I walked <u>down</u> the winding <u>street</u>.
The girl <u>with</u> red <u>hair</u> is an artist.

In the first sentence, the preposition is the word *down.* The object is *street.* The entire phrase is *down the winding street.* The two important words in the phrase are the preposition *down* and the object *street.*

In the second sentence, the preposition is *with* and the object is *hair.* The prepositional phrase is the group of words, *with red hair.*

In grammar, a **phrase** is a group of words, *without a subject and predicate*, that functions as *a single part of speech.* A prepositional phrase is a phrase that functions as an *adjective* or an *adverb.* Since adjectives and adverbs are modifiers, the prepositional phrase is also a modifier.

ADJECTIVE PHRASES

An *adjective phrase* is a prepositional phrase that modifies a *noun* or a *pronoun.* An adjective phrase is often the equivalent of an adjective, as you will readily see from the following illustrations:

The man *at the gate* sold us the tickets.
We followed the path *near the river*.

In the first sentence, the prepositional phrase is *at the gate*. It is an adjective phrase because it modifies the noun *man*. The phrase, *at the gate*, is the equivalent of an adjective because it means the *gate* man.

In the second sentence, the prepositional phrase is *near the river*. This is also an adjective phrase because it modifies the noun *path*. The sentence means that we followed the *river* path. The phrase *near the river* is the equivalent of an adjective.

Like the adjective, the adjective phrase *describes* or *limits* the noun or pronoun which it modifies.

She wore a hat *with blue trimming*. (describes the hat)
He lives in the house *to your right*. (limited to a particular house)

An adjective phrase may follow the noun which it modifies, or it may be used in the predicate after a linking verb.

The accident *on the bridge* was not serious. (follows the noun)
The injured man seemed *in a daze*. (follows a linking verb)

You will not acquire skill in recognizing prepositional phrases unless you become familiar with the words that are commonly used as prepositions. This list appeared in Chapter Two, and it is repeated here for reference. Refer to this list until you are able to identify the prepositions that are in common use.

Commonly Used Prepositions

above	at	by	into	toward
about	before	down	like	through
across	behind	during	near	under
after	below	except	of	until
against	beneath	for	off	up
among	between	in	since	with
around	but (except)	inside	to	within

The fact that a word appears in this list does not mean that

153

it is always used as a preposition. Many of the words that are commonly used as prepositions are also used as adverbs.

Planes were flying *above the city*. (*Above* is a preposition.)
Planes were flying *above*. (*Above* is an adverb.)

ADVERBIAL PHRASES

An *adverbial phrase* is a prepositional phrase that modifies a *verb*, an *adjective*, or an *adverb*. Like the adverb, the adverbial phrase answers the questions: *when? where? how?* and *to what extent?* Adverbial phrases express *time, place, manner,* and *degree*.

I shall return *at noon*. (Phrase expresses *time*.)
The sailor was working *on the deck*. (Phrase expresses *place*.)
Tell the story *in your own words*. (Phrase expresses *manner*.)

In the first sentence, the adverbial phrase is *at noon*. The phrase tells *when* or at what time I shall return. It modifies the verb *shall return*. The adverbial phrase in the second sentence is *on the deck*. This phrase tells *where* or *at what place* the sailor was working. It modifies the verb *was working*. The adverbial phrase in the third sentence is *in your own words*. It tells *how* or *in what manner* you should tell the story. The phrase modifies the verb *tell*.

Adverbial phrases that modify verbs are very easy to identify. Those that modify adjectives and adverbs are not always easy to identify. The adverbial phrase that modifies an adjective usually follows that adjective. Study the following illustration carefully:

The child seemed afraid *of the noise*. (modifies *afraid*)

In this sentence, the adverbial phrase *of the noise* modifies the predicate adjective *afraid*. Adverbial phrases that modify adjectives usually follow this pattern.

COMPOUND OR PHRASAL PREPOSITIONS

A preposition is not always a single word. There are a number of prepositions in common use that are made up of a group of two or more words. Such prepositions are called **compound prepositions** or **phrasal prepositions**.

Although the *compound preposition* consists of two or more words, it is regarded as a unit, or as a single preposition. The following list includes the compound prepositions that are in common use:

according to
along side of
along with
because of
by means of
by reason of
by way of
contrary to
for the sake of
in addition to
in accordance with
in case of

in consideration of
in apposition with
in front of
in regard to
in respect to
in spite of
instead of
on account of
out of
with reference to
with regard to
with respect to

Compound Prepositions in Sentences

In compliance with his request, we closed the account.
According to our schedule, the job will be completed tomorrow.
The president resigned *on account of illness*.

PRONOUNS USED AS OBJECT OF PREPOSITIONS

You have already learned that the object of a preposition is always in the **objective case.** When nouns are used as objects

155

of prepositions, they do not present a problem because nouns do not have different forms for the objective case.

Pronouns do present a problem in case because some of the *personal pronouns* and the pronoun *who* have one form for the nominative case and another form for the objective case. When a pronoun is used as the object of a preposition, the form for the objective case must be used.

It is incorrect to use the forms *I, he, she, we, they,* or *who* as objects of prepositions. They are **nominative case** forms. The correct forms to use are *me, him, her, us, them,* and *whom.* In the following sentences, all the pronouns that are used as objects of prepositions are in the **objective case:**

The speaker spoke to **me** after the meeting. (*me*—objective case)

I went to the Art Institute with **her.** (*her*—objective case)

We looked at **him** while he was dancing. (*him*—objective case)

The women prepared a dinner for **them.** (*them*—objective case)

The librarian found the books for **us.** (*us*—objective case)

For **whom** are you working now? (*whom*—objective case)

Watch the two words, *but* and *like,* carefully when they are followed by pronouns. The word *but* is a preposition when it means *except.* When the word *but* is used as a preposition, it must be followed by the objective case. Similarly, when the word *like* is used as a preposition, it must be followed by the objective case of the pronoun. As a preposition, *like* means *similar to,* or *in a manner similar to.* (Other uses of the word *like* will be found in Chapter 19.)

No one knew the answer **but** me. (*but*—preposition)

His son looks **like** him. (*like*—preposition)

THE CORRECT USE OF PREPOSITIONS

Many of the common prepositions are often used incorrectly. Since a preposition expresses a relationship between the object and some other word in the sentence, the preposition that you use must be selected with care. Very often the speaker or writer is not aware of the distinctions in meaning that careful writers and speakers observe in using prepositions. The following are some of the prepositions that you should use with discrimination.

Differences in Meaning

1. **Around, about.** *Around* means encircling. *About* often means approximately. Do not use *around* when you mean approximately.

The fish weighed *around* three pounds. (incorrect)
The fish weighed *about* two pounds. (correct)
She tied a ribbon *about* her head. (incorrect)
She tied a ribbon *around* her head. (correct)

2. **Agree to, agree with.** One *agrees to* a proposal, but *agrees with* a person.

The members *agreed with* the president. (correct—*person*)
I *agree to* your plan for saving money. (correct—*proposal*)

3. **Beside, besides.** *Beside* means by the side of. *Besides* means in addition to.

Margaret sat *beside* her father. (*by the side of*)
There were three *besides* Jerry in the boat. (*in addition to*)

4. **Between, among.** *Between* is used when referring to two. *Among* is used when referring to more than two.

Frank and Harry divided the money *between* them. (*two persons*)
The money was divided *among* the five heirs. (*more than two*)

5. **Differ with, differ from.** One differs *with a person* in the matter of opinion. A person or thing *differs from* another in certain respects; that is, the person or thing is *unlike* another in certain respects.

I *differ with* you about his qualifications. (*matter of opinion*)
Maine *differs from* Florida in many ways. (*in certain respects*)

6. **Different from, different than.** *Different from* is correct. Do not use *different than*, which is incorrect.

The motion picture is *different from* the book. (correct)
The motion picture is *different than* the book. (incorrect)

7. **In, into.** The preposition *in* indicates location or motion within a place. *Into* indicates motion *toward the inside* of a place from the outside.

The tea was held *in* the garden. (*within a place*)
The swimmer jumped *into* the pool. (*from the outside*)
He swam *in* the pool. (*motion within a place*)

8. **In back of, behind.** *In back of* should never be used for *behind*.

The car is *in back* of the house. (incorrect)
The car is *behind* the house. (correct)

9. **Over, more than.** *Over* expresses the idea of *place*. *More than* expresses the idea of *quantity*.

The actress has *over* a hundred dresses. (incorrect)
The actress has *more than* a hundred dresses. (correct)
She wore a cape *over* her shoulders. (correct—*place*)

10. **Outside of, except.** Do not use *outside of* when you mean *except*.

No one went *outside of* James. (incorrect)
No one went *except* James. (correct)

11. **To, too.** The preposition *to* should not be confused with the adverb *too*.

I am going *to* the Dunes. (preposition *to*)
Will you go, *too*? (adverb, meaning *also*)

12. **Within, inside of.** Do not use *inside of* to express time. Use *within*.

He will leave *inside of* a week. (incorrect)
He will leave *within* a week. (correct)

13. **In regard to, with regard to.** Do not say *in regards to* or *with regards to*. The correct expressions are *in regard to* and *with regard to*.

In regards to your order (incorrect)
In regard to your order (correct)

14. **Unnecessary prepositions.** Do not use *off of* for *off*. The *of* should not be added. Always omit the unnecessary prepositions in sentences like the following:

He jumped *off of* the pier. (*of* is superfluous)
He jumped *off* the pier. (correct)
Where is he *at*? (incorrect)
Where is he? (correct)
Where is he going *to*? (incorrect)
Where is he going? (correct)
Is the rain over *with*? (incorrect)
Is the rain over? (correct)

POSITION OF THE PREPOSITION

Many persons believe that it is incorrect to end a sentence with a preposition. Very often it is more natural and more emphatic to place the preposition at the end of the sentence. In many questions, the preposition comes naturally at the end. But a preposition should not be used at the end of a sentence if it sounds awkward or changes the meaning of the sentence. The following sentences end with a preposition. The prepositions fall naturally and correctly at the end.

Whom are you looking *for*?

What kind of plane is he traveling *in*?
They sold the car you were looking *at*.

Ordinarily, the preposition should not be placed at the end of the sentence. However, many of our best writers and speakers occasionally end sentences in this way.

17. THE COMPOUND SENTENCE

Chapter Four explained that there are four types of sentences: *declarative*, *interrogative*, *imperative*, and *exclamatory sentences*. A particular sentence falls into one of these groups according to the purpose which it serves.

When you make a statement, you use a declarative sentence, but when you ask a question, you use an interrogative sentence. If your purpose is to issue a command or make a request, you use the imperative sentence. When you want to express strong feeling or sudden emotion, you use an exclamatory sentence.

KINDS OF CLAUSES

There is still another way of classifying sentences. This classification is based upon the internal structure of the sentence or the way in which it is built up. Thus far, we have been dealing with the sentence that has the simplest form of internal structure——the *simple sentence*. We have been dealing with the simple sentence because our chief problem has been the relationships that words have to each other.

In this unit you will begin a study of the more complicated sentence patterns. You will learn how to build up sentences in a number of different ways. This knowledge will enable you to express your ideas in a variety of ways and will give you more power over language.

The type of classification of sentences which you will study is based upon the *number* and *kinds* of **clauses** which a sentence contains. According to this classification, sentences are divided into four groups: *simple, compound, complex*, and *compound complex*. In this unit we shall limit our study to the simple sentence and the compound sentence.

Before you can understand the difference between a simple sentence and a compound sentence, you must have a very clear idea of what is meant by a clause in grammar.

A **clause** is a group of words that has a *subject* and a *predicate*. There are two kinds of clauses: *independent* or *main* clauses and *dependent* or *subordinate* clauses.

INDEPENDENT CLAUSES

An **independent clause** is a group of words that has a subject and a predicate. An independent clause does not depend upon anything else for its meaning. It expresses a complete thought. An independent clause is a simple sentence when it stands alone.

The officer blew his whistle and the cars stopped.

In this sentence, there are two independent clauses. The first independent clause is *The officer blew his whistle*. The second independent clause is *the cars stopped*. These clauses could be written as two simple sentences by omitting the conjunction *and*. The conjunction *and* does not belong to either of the independent clauses. It simple brings the two independent clauses together in one sentence.

The officer blew his whistle. The cars stopped.

SUBORDINATE CLAUSES

A **subordinate clause** is a group of words that has a subject and a predicate, *but the clause cannot stand alone*. A subordinate clause does not express a complete thought. It depends upon the main clause for its meaning. The connective, or the word that introduces the subordinate clause, plays an important part in making it a dependent clause. In the following sentence the subordinate clause is underlined.

The cars stopped <u>when the officer blew his whistle.</u>

In this sentence, the group of words, *when the officer blew his whistle*, is a subordinate clause. It cannot stand alone although it has both a subject and a predicate. The word *when*, which introduces the clause, makes the words which follow it dependent upon the main clause for the meaning. That is the reason why the clause, *when the officer blew his whistle*, is called a dependent or a subordinate clause.

The group of words, *the cars stopped*, is an independent clause. It could stand alone. It is the main clause in the sentence because it states the main idea in the sentence.

THE SIMPLE SENTENCE

A **simple sentence** is a sentence having *one* subject and *one* predicate, either or both of which may be *compound*. A simple sentence consists of one and only one independent clause. All of the following sentences are simple sentences, but some have compound subjects or predicates. The last sentence has both a compound subject and a compound predicate.

<u>John</u> <u>joined</u> the Navy. (simple subject and predicate)
<u>John</u> and <u>Fred</u> <u>joined</u> the Marines. (compound subject)
<u>Mary</u> <u>sang</u> and <u>played</u> at the concert. (compound predicate)
<u>Mary</u> and <u>Jane</u> <u>sang</u> and <u>played</u> at the concert. (compound subject and predicate)

Note that a compound subject does not mean two subjects. It means the *one* subject is made up of two or more nouns or pronouns. A *compound predicate* does not mean two predicates. It means that *one* predicate is made up of two or more verbs or verb phrases.

THE COMPOUND SENTENCE

A **compound sentence** is a sentence that *contains two or more independent clauses*. The independent clauses of a compound sentence must be joined in some way to indicate that the independent clauses form one sentence.

163

When you put two independent clauses or two simple sentences together to form one longer sentence, you have a compound sentence:

John joined the Navy. (simple sentence)
Harry joined the Marines. (simple sentence)

If you join these two simple sentences in order to make a compound sentence, you have the problem of punctuation and the problem of using a conjunction. The following sentences show the ways in which two simple sentences might be joined to form one compound sentence:

John joined the Navy, **but** Harry joined the Marines. (*comma* and *conjunction*)
John joined the Navy; Harry joined the Marines. (*semicolon*)
John joined the Navy **but** Harry joined the Marines. (*conjunction only*)

From these illustrations you can see that the independent clauses of a compound sentence may be connected in one of three ways:

1. By using a comma before a conjunction
2. By using a semicolon without a conjunction
3. By using a conjunction without a comma

All three methods of writing a compound sentence are correct. However, you will use the first method, a comma before a conjunction, much more frequently than the other two methods. You will learn more about each method of punctuation as you progress in this unit.

IDENTIFYING THE COMPOUND SENTENCE

Some persons have difficulty in distinguishing between a simple sentence with a compound subject or predicate, and a compound sentence. The point to keep in mind is that the compound sentence must be the equivalent of at least *two complete simple sentences*. Examine the following illustration carefully:

The Indian squaw cooks, sews, and builds the wigwam.

This is not a compound sentence. It is a simple sentence with a compound predicate. You could not possibly make two independent clauses out of the sentence as it is written. In order to turn it into a compound sentence, you would have to supply another subject and write the sentence as two independent clauses:

The Indian squaw cooks and sews, **and** she builds the wigwam.

COORDINATE CONJUNCTIONS

The independent clauses of a compound sentence are often connected by a coordinate conjunction. **Coordinate** means of the *same rank* or *of equal rank*. **Coordinate conjunctions** are used to connect words, phrases, and clauses of equal rank. The independent clauses of a compound sentence are of the same rank; therefore, we use a coordinate conjunction to connect them. The coordinate conjunctions that are commonly used for this purpose are *for, and, but, or, not,* and *while* when it means the same as *but*.

Use of the Comma and Coordinate Conjunction

When a coordinate conjunction is used in a compound sentence, it is usually preceded by a comma. The comma should not be omitted unless the independent clauses are very short and the thought is closely connected. Observe the use of the comma and the coordinate conjunction in each of the following compound sentences. The independent clauses are underlined.
Arthur washed our new car, **and** Ned polished it.
I may consider your plan, **or** I may disregard it.

I did not seek the position, **nor** do I want it.

Michael likes tennis, **but** he prefers to play golf.

Their team was untrained, **while** ours was highly trained.

Jack went to bed early, **for** he was very tired.

In modern writing, the comma is often omitted before the conjunctions *and* and *or*. Careful writers, however, usually place a comma before the conjunctions *but* and *for*. If a comma is not placed before the word *for* when it is used as a coordinate conjunction, *for* might be mistaken for a preposition.

USE OF THE SEMICOLON IN THE COMPOUND SENTENCE

You have learned that a comma and a coordinate conjunction are often used to separate the clauses of a compound sentence. Sometimes the ideas combined in a compound sentence are so closely related that it is not necessary to use a conjunction. In that case, a semicolon is used to separate the two clauses. The following are two important uses of the semicolon in the compound sentence:

1. A semicolon should be used between the independent clauses of a compound sentence *when they are not joined by a coordinate conjunction*. In the following sentence, there is no conjunction between the two independent clauses; therefore, a semicolon is used.

The doctor came in late; he did not stop to read the telegram.

2. When the independent clauses of a compound sentence are very long, or have *internal punctuation*, a semicolon is generally used before the coordinate conjunction. **Internal punctuation** means that there are commas within one or both of the independent clauses.

Shakespeare, a great dramatist, wrote a great many plays; and he also wrote a number of sonnets.

166

Temperamental and lazy, John managed to get along without
    working; but he was never contented or happy.

Both of these sentences have one or more commas in the
first independent clause; that is, the first clause has *internal
punctuation*. A semicolon is used between the two independent
clauses even though a coordinate conjunction is used.

THE "COMMA FAULT"

You have just learned that two independent clauses may be
joined by a semicolon when no conjunction is used. You have
also learned that two independent clauses are often joined by
a coordinate conjunction and a comma. The point to keep in
mind is that two independent clauses should not be joined by
a comma unless a coordinate conjunction is used. When a writer
uses a comma between the independent clauses of a compound
sentence, he makes an error known as the "comma fault."
The following sentence illustrates the "comma fault."

The author wrote many stories for children, she also wrote a
    number of historical novels. (*comma fault*)

In this sentence, two independent clauses are joined by means
of a comma. This is known as the "comma fault" because the
comma is the sole connection between two independent clauses.
This error may be eliminated by punctuating the sentence in
any one of the three ways that have been given in this unit:

1. Use a coordinate conjunction after the comma:

The author wrote many stories for children, and she also wrote
    a number of historical novels. (*correct*)

2. Use a semicolon between the two independent clauses:

The author wrote many stories for children; she also wrote a
    number of historical novels. (*correct*)

3. Punctuate the two independent clauses as two simple sentences:

The author wrote many stories for children. She also wrote a number of historical novels. (*correct*)

A skillful writer sometimes puts commas between the independent clauses of a compound sentence. This is done deliberately for the purpose of producing a certain effect. The clauses are usually very short and similar in length and structure. The following sentence is a famous example:

"I came, I saw, I conquered.'

THE RUN ON SENTENCE

The **run on sentence error** is very similar to the "*comma fault.*" The only difference is that the run on sentence consists of two or more independent statements that are run together without any mark of punctuation, or without any connecting word. The following sentence is an illustration of the run on sentence:

Money provided by stockholders has helped the company purchase equipment and supplies it has also enabled the company to expand its production.

In this sentence, two independent statements have been run together without any punctuation or without any connecting word or words. The sentence might be correctly written by following any of the suggestions civen for removing the "*comma fault.*"

Since the run on sentence error is commonly made, you should check your writing carefully. Be sure that you do not run sentences together without punctuation or proper connectives.

TRANSITIONAL WORDS

There is another type of connecting word that you may use between the independent clauses of a compound sentence. The words that belong in this group are not coordinate conjunctions. They are sometimes called **transitional words** because they are not pure conjunctions.

Some of these words have a slight connecting force. Others have some adverbial force. But they all belong to the independent clause which they introduce or in which they are found. Connectives that belong to this group *are always preceded by a semicolon*.

Since many of these words are regarded as independent elements, they are usually set off by commas. Words like *moreover, however, therefore*, and *nevertheless* are usually set off. Words like *then, still, yet*, and *so* are seldom set off by commas when they retain their adverbial force.

Sometimes the connection is made by a group of words. Expressions like the following are transitional words and are regarded as a single connecting word: *in fact, on the other hand, that is*, etc. Study the following illustrations carefully:

The road was unpaved; **nevertheless,** we drove on in the rain.

I missed the first boat; **however,** I arrived on time.

The president introduced the speaker; **then** he sat down.

Ethel was sick; **in fact,** she had one of her usual colds.

We arrived early; **as a result,** we had time to visit with our friends.

We cannot get materials; **consequently,** we cannot finish the job.

I became tired of doing his work; **moreover,** I had my own work to do.

I did not dislike the play; **on the contrary,** I enjoyed it immensely.

On the page following is a list of commonly used transitional words.

Commonly Used Transitional Words

Following is a list of transitional words which are used frequently. Become familiar with them.

accordingly	indeed	as a result
afterwards	likewise	at last
again	meanwhile	at the same time
anyhow	moreover	for example
besides	namely	for instance
consequently	nevertheless	for this reason
doubtless	next	in any case
eventually	otherwise	in fact
evidently	perhaps	in like manner
finally	possibly	in short
furthermore	still	on the contrary
hence	then	on the other hand
however	therefore	that is
yet	thus	in addition

18. THE COMPLEX SENTENCE

Chapter 17 explained how to form a compound sentence by combining two or more simple sentences into one longer sentence. It also explained how to punctuate the compound sentence when a coordinate conjunction is used, when transitional words are used, and when no conjunction is used.

The compound sentence is an important type of sentence because it enables us to combine two or more related ideas. However, it is just as ineffective to use a number of compound sentences strung along with *ands* and *buts* as it is to use a number of short, choppy sentences.

In this unit you will learn how to use a type of sentence that will enable you to put less important ideas in subordinate positions in the sentence. This type of sentence is called the *complex sentence*.

A **complex sentence** is a sentence that consists of one *independent clause* and *one or more subordinate clauses*. *Subordinate* means lower in rank, power, or importance. A subordinate clause is less important than an independent clause because it depends upon the independent clause for its meaning. The independent clause is also called the *main* or the *principal* clause. An independent clause is a group of words that has a subject and a predicate, and does not depend upon anything else for its meaning. It expresses a complete thought, and can stand alone.

A **subordinate clause** is a group of words that has a subject and a predicate, but *cannot stand alone*. A subordinate clause does not express a complete thought. It should never be punctuated as if it were a complete sentence.

A subordinate clause is usually introduced by some type of *subordinate conjunction* or by a *relative pronoun*. These connecting words make it clear that the clause expresses an idea that is subordinate to the main clause. They also join the subordinate clause to some word in the independent clause. In the following sentences, the independent clauses and the subordinate clauses are underlined.

Complex Sentences

I shall be at the station when you arrive.
I shall not go to the park if it rains.
She wore a beautiful dress which her grandmother had worn.

In the first sentence, the subordinate clause is *when you arrive*. The clause is introduced by the **subordinate conjunction** *when*. The group of words, *when you arrive*, has a subject and a predicate, but it cannot stand alone. That is the reason why the clause is called a *subordinate clause*. It depends upon the main clause for its meaning.

The subordinate clause in the second sentence is *if it rains*. This group of words cannot stand alone. The clause is introduced by the subordinate conjunction *if*. This conjunction helps the subordinate clause express the idea that there is a condition upon which *my going* depends.

The subordinate clause in the third sentence is *which her grandmother had worn*. This clause is introduced by the relative pronoun *which*. The word *which* refers to the word *dress* in the independent clause. It also introduces the subordinate clause. A **relative pronoun** always joins a clause to the *antecedent* of the pronoun. In this sentence, the antecedent of the relative pronoun is *dress*. *Dress* is the word to which the pronoun refers.

The relative pronoun also has an important function in the subordinate clause. It might be the subject of the clause, the object of the verb in the clause, the object of a preposition, or a predicate pronoun after a linking verb.

KINDS OF SUBORDINATE CLAUSES

There are three kinds of subordinate clauses: *adverbial clauses*, *adjective clauses*, and *noun clauses*. Each of these different types is used as a part of speech. That is why subordinate clauses are called adverbial clauses, adjective clauses, and noun clauses.

The **adverbial clause** functions as an adverb. The **adjective clause** functions as an adjective, and the **noun clause** functions as a noun.

Adverbs modify verbs, adjectives, and other adverbs. Adverbial clauses also modify verbs, adjectives, and adverbs. Adjectives modify nouns and pronouns. Adjective clauses also modify nouns and pronouns. Nouns are used as subjects of sentences, as objects of verbs, and as objects of prepositions. Noun clauses are used in the same ways.

Subordinate Clauses

The man who received the medal was my uncle. (adjective clause)

We always stop working when the bell rings. (adverbial clause)

I believe that the bookkeeper is honest. (noun clause)

In the first sentence, the subordinate clause is the group of words, *who received the medal*. The subordinate clause is an **adjective clause** and modifies the word *man*. In the second sentence, the subordinate clause is *when the bell rings*. It is an **adverbial clause** and modifies the verb *stop*. This clause expresses *time* just as an adverb expresses *time*. The subordinate clause in the third sentence is the group of words, *that the bookkeeper is honest*. This subordinate clause is a **noun clause** and is used as the object of the verb *believe*.

ADJECTIVE CLAUSES

An **adjective clause** *is a subordinate clause that functions as an adjective.* Adjectives are used to describe or limit nouns or pronouns. An adjective clause is also used to describe or limit a noun or a pronoun.

An adjective clause is usually introduced by a relative pronoun. A **relative pronoun** *is a pronoun that joins an adjective clause to some word in the independent or main clause*. The word to which it joins the clause is the *antecedent* of the relative pronoun. The relative pronouns used in this way are *who* (*whom*), *which*, and *that*.

Adjective Clauses Introduced by Relative Pronouns

John brought the books that you ordered. (*that* — relative pronoun)

I favored the plan which the senator proposed. (*which*—relative pronoun)

Men who are thinkers look for facts. (*who*—relative pronoun)

I saw the salesman whom I met at the office. (*whom*—relative pronoun)

The subordinate clause in the first sentence is *that you ordered*. It is an adjective clause and modifies the noun *books*. This clause is introduced by the relative pronoun *that*. The antecedent of the relative pronoun *that* is the word *books*. The pronoun *that* joins its clause to the word *books* in the main clause.

The subordinate clause in the second sentence is *which the senator proposed*. It is an adjective clause and modifies the noun *plan*. The antecedent of the relative pronoun *which* is the word *plan*. The adjective clause limits the meaning to the *plan which the senator proposed*.

The subordinate clause in the third sentence is *who are thinkers*. The main clause is *Men look for facts*. In this sentence the subordinate clause comes between the subject and the predicate of the main clause. The subordinate clause is introduced by the relative pronoun *who*. The antecedent of *who* is *men*.

The adjective clause in the fourth sentence is *whom I met at the office*. This clause is introduced by the relative pronoun *whom*. The antecedent of the pronoun is the word *salesman*.

Relative Adjectives

Sometimes an adjective clause is introduced by the word *whose*, which is the possessive form of the pronoun *who*. In such cases the word *whose* modifies a noun which follows it. When the word *whose* is used in an adjective clause, it is called a **relative adjective.** The word *relative* is used to show that the word *whose* refers to its antecedent in the main clause.

That is the *man* **whose** car was stolen. (*man*—antecedent)

In this sentence the word *whose* is a relative adjective, modifying the word *car*. The antecedent of *whose* is the word *man* in the main clause. The word *whose* connects the clause *whose car was stolen* to the word *man*.

Adjective Clauses Introduced by Relative Adverbs

Adjective clauses are often introduced by the relative adverbs *where, when*, and *why*. When these adverbs introduce adjective clauses they relate to some word in the main clause in much the same way as a relative pronoun does. A relative adverb always has an antecedent and joins its clause to that antecedent. In addition, a relative adverb performs the function of an adverb in its own clause. It is called a *relative adverb* because it relates to an antecedent.

I found the house where the poet lived. (*where*—relative adverb)

The doctor selected a time when I was not working. (*when*—relative adverb)

I discovered the reason why he is leaving. (*why*—relative adverb)

In the first sentence, the relative adverb is *where*. It introduces the clause, *where the poet lived*. It also refers to its antecedent, *house*. As an adverb, it modifies the verb *lived* in the subordinate clause.

The relative adverb in the second sentence is *when*. Its antecedent is *time*. The relative adverb *when* joins the clause, *when I was not working*, to its antecedent *time*. It also functions as an adverb, modifying the verb *was working*.

The relative adverb in the third sentence is *why*. Its antecedent is *reason*. It modifies the verb *is leaving* in its own clause.

The only difference between a relative adverb and a simple adverb is the fact that the relative adverb is found in an adjective clause and refers to its antecedent in the main clause. Both relative adverbs and simple adverbs modify verbs.

"WHO" AND "WHOM" IN SUBORDINATE CLAUSES

It is often difficult to determine whether to use "who" or "whom" when one of these words is used to introduce a subordinate clause. Always keep in mind that *who* is the correct form for the nominative case, and *whom* is the correct form for the objective case.

When a relative pronoun introduces a clause, it has a double function. It joins the clause to its antecedent which is in the main clause, and in addition it performs one of the following three functions in the subordinate clause:

1. The pronoun may be the *subject* of the subordinate clause.
2. The pronoun may be used as a *predicate pronoun* after a linking verb.
3. The pronoun may be used as the *object* of the verb or a preposition.

In order to determine how the pronoun is used, it is often necessary to put the subordinate clause in grammatical order, or to transpose it.

Allen was the one *who published the report*. (*who*—subject)

In this sentence, it is clear that *who* is the subject of the subordinate clause. The form *who* is correct because the subject is in the nominative case.

The president is a man *whom everyone admires*. (*whom*—direct object)

In this sentence, the word *whom* is the direct object of the verb *admires*. By transposing the clause, you will be able to see this clearly: *everyone admires whom*. The subject of the clause is *everyone*, not *whom*.

Jack is the boy *to whom they gave the camera*. (*whom*—object of preposition)

In this sentence, the pronoun *whom* is the object of the preposition *to*. When the subordinate clause is transposed, the use of *whom* becomes clear: *they gave the camera to whom*. *They* is the subject of the clause, not *whom*.

RESTRICTIVE AND NONRESTRICTIVE CLAUSES

Adjective clauses present a problem in meaning and in punctuation. Sometimes the adjective clause is set off by commas. Sometimes the adjective clause is not set off by commas. The following sentences are illustrations of adjective clauses that are *not* set off by commas:

I spoke to the woman *who was giving the demonstration*.
This is the man *who discovered the leak in the pipe*.
I dislike driving in a town *where there are no stop signals*.

In the first sentence, the adjective clause is *who was giving the demonstration*. If you leave the clause out, the meaning of the sentence is changed. The sentence now gives no indication of *who* the woman was. Since the clause identifies that woman, it is essential to the meaning of the sentence.

In the second sentence, the clause is *who discovered the leak in the pipe*. This clause identifies the man and is essential to the meaning of the sentence. The clause restricts the meaning of the sentence to the man *who discovered the leak in the pipe*. Therefore, it is essential to the meaning of the sentence.

The third sentence does not mean that *I dislike driving in a town*. The meaning is restricted to driving in a certain type of town; that is, in a town *where there are no stop signals*.

Clauses that are necessary to the meaning of the sentence are called *restrictive clauses*. A restrictive clause is not set off by commas. A **restrictive clause** identifies the word it modifies.

Some adjective clauses are not essential to the meaning of the sentence. They give added information, but the essential meaning of the sentence would not be changed if such clauses were omitted. Study the following sentences carefully:

Mr. Miller, *who lived next door*, moved to Canada.
Will James, *who was once a cowboy*, wrote many stories.
Father, *who was working in the garden*, missed the broadcast.
The speaker, *who was accompanied by his wife*, left early.

In the first sentence, the clause, *who lived next door*, gives additional information about Mr. Miller, but the meaning of the sentence is not changed if you leave the clause out. The clause does not place any restrictions on the meaning. Therefore it is called a *nonrestrictive clause*. Nonrestrictive clauses are set off by commas.

A **nonrestrictive clause** is a subordinate clause that is *not* essential to the meaning of the sentence. All the clauses in the preceding illustrations are nonrestrictive clauses. They are set off by commas. They are not needed in the sentence to identify the person who is mentioned in the main clause.

A nonrestrictive clause functions more like an appositive or a parenthetical expression. You might call it a thrown in remark. That is the reason why the nonrestrictive clause is set off by commas.

19. ADVERBIAL CLAUSES

Chapter Eighteen explained that an adjective clause functions in the same way as an adjective functions. Adjectives modify nouns and pronouns. Adjective clauses also modify nouns and pronouns.

An *adverbial clause* functions in the same way as an adverb functions. Adverbs tell *how, when, where*, and *to what extent* the action is performed. Adverbial clauses answer the same questions and, in addition, express several other ideas which the simple adverb does not express.

Adverbs modify verbs, adjectives, and other adverbs. Adverbial clauses also modify verbs, adjectives, and adverbs. The adverbial clause modifies a verb more often than it modifies an adjective or an adverb.

SUBORDINATE CONJUNCTIONS

An adverbial clause is usually introduced by a *subordinate conjunction*. This connecting word is called a subordinate conjunction because it makes the idea expressed by its clause *subordinate to the main idea in the sentence*. The subordinate conjunction also shows the relation between the subordinate clause and the word in the main clause which the subordinate clause modifies.

The **subordinate conjunction** is used to show that the clause which it introduces is a subordinate clause, and not a main clause. The subordinate conjunction also indicates the exact type of relationship that the subordinate clause has to the main clause.

The following illustrations will make clear the function of the *subordinate conjunction* in a subordinate clause:

We listened to the radio because we wanted to hear the news.

(adverbial clause—modifies listened)

She <u>will find</u> the telegram on her desk <u>when she returns</u>. (adverbial clause—modifies <u>will find</u>)

In the first sentence, the subordinate clause is *because we wanted to hear the news*. It is an adverbial clause and modifies the verb *listened* in the main clause. The subordinate conjunction is the word *because*.

If you leave out the word *because*, the words that follow no longer express a subordinate idea. They express a complete thought. It is the word *because* that makes the group of words, *we wanted to hear the news*, subordinate to the main clause. The **subordinate conjunction** is the key to the adverbial clause.

You should become familiar with the subordinate conjunctions that are commonly used to introduce *adverbial clauses*. The subordinate conjunction will help you identify the adverbial clause. It will also help you determine the **kind** of adverbial clause which it introduces.

WORDS USED AS SUBORDINATE CONJUNCTIONS

after	even though,	till
although	except	though
as	if	unless
as—as	in order that	until
as if	provided	when
as long as	provided that	whenever
as soon as	since	where
as though	so—as	wherever
because	so that	whether
before	than	while
even if	that	

KINDS OF ADVERBIAL CLAUSES

Adverbial clauses are used to express a number of different ideas. The following are the ten important ideas which are expressed by adverbial clauses: *time, place, manner, degree, comparison, purpose, result, condition, concession, cause (reason).*

Since the subordinate conjunction helps the adverbial clause express the idea intended, you should become familiar with the conjunctions that are used to express certain ideas, such as *time, place*, etc. The following is a list of the subordinate conjunctions commonly used in adverbial clauses of the various types:

Time: after, before, when, whenever, since, until, as soon as, while

Place: where, wherever

Manner: as, as if, as though

Degree: that, as—as, not so—as, than

Comparison: as, than, so—as, as—as

Purpose: that, so that, in order that

Result: that, so that

Condition: if, provided, provided that, unless

Concession: although, though, even if

Cause: as, because, since

Ideas Expressed by Adverbial Clauses

Time: I watched the crowd <u>while I was waiting for you.</u>

Place: Put the notice <u>where it can be seen.</u>

Manner: The soldier walks <u>as if he were lame.</u>

Degree: Marvin is not so industrious <u>as his brother (is industrious).</u>

Comparison: The train was later <u>than it usually is.</u>

Purpose: Ted practiced every day <u>so that he might win the contest.</u>

Result: The salesman was so persuasive <u>that I finally bought the car.</u>

Condition: I shall attend the meeting <u>if I have the time.</u>

181

Concession: Frances will sing at the concert <u>although she has a cold.</u>

Cause or Reason: Gerald read the book <u>because I recommended it.</u>

CLAUSES OF DEGREE

An *adverbial clause of degree* that is introduced by the subordinate conjunction *that* usually expresses a **result** idea as well as the idea of **degree**. The degree idea is expressed by words like *such*, *such a*, and *so* which precede the subordinate clause.

Jane practiced <u>so</u> long <u>that she became very tired.</u>
Harold made <u>such</u> a poor sales record <u>that he lost his position.</u>

In both these sentences, the adverbial clauses introduced by *that* express a *degree idea* and a *result idea.*

An adverbial clause of degree usually modifies an adjective or an adverb in the main clause.

He talked <u>so</u> loud <u>that he annoyed the speaker.</u>

In this sentence, the adverbial clause *that he annoyed the speaker* is introduced by the subordinate conjunction *that*. The adverbial clause modifies the adverb *so* in the main clause.

THE POSITION OF
THE ADVERBIAL CLAUSE

In all of the preceding illustrations, the adverbial clause follows the main clause. An adverbial clause is often placed at the beginning of the sentence for emphasis, or for variety in sentence patterns. When the subordinate clause precedes the main clause, it is usually set off by a comma.

He went to the office <u>when it was convenient.</u> (follows main clause)

When it was convenient, he went to the office. (precedes main clause)

The men work overtime whenever it is necessary. (follows main clause)

Whenever it is necessary, the men work overtime. (precedes main clause)

In the first sentence, the adverbial clause *follows* the main clause. In the second sentence, the same adverbial clause *precedes* the main clause. The adverbial clause is placed at the beginning of the sentence for emphasis. Since the adverbial clause is in inverted or transposed order, it is set off by a comma.

The adverbial clause in the third sentence *follows* the main clause. In the fourth sentence, this same clause is placed at the beginning of the sentence for emphasis. The adverbial clause is set off by a comma because it is in transposed order.

Sometimes it is necessary to change the position of a noun and a pronoun when the adverbial clause is placed at the beginning of a sentence:

I shall visit **Margaret** in Texas if she sends me her address.
If Margaret sends me her address, I shall visit **her** in Texas.

CLAUSES OF COMPARISON

In both speaking and writing, words are often omitted that are necessary to the grammatical completeness of the sentence. Certain words are sometimes omitted because the meaning of the sentence is perfectly clear without them. Sometimes they are omitted in order to avoid using a sentence that is awkward or monotonous.

Certain words are usually omitted in an *adverbial clause of comparison* for the reasons just given. The verb is often omitted because it can be readily supplied. It is important to realize that the verb has been omitted in order to decide upon

183

the correct form of the pronoun that should be used as the subject of the verb. We often hear sentences like the following, which are incorrect:

I am younger than **him.** (incorrect)
John can run as fast as **us.** (incorrect)

In both sentences the *incorrect form* of the pronoun is used in the adverbial clause of comparison. If the speaker had finished the clause, he would have used the correct form of the pronoun. When the clause is finished, it becomes evident that the pronoun is the *subject* of the clause. A pronoun used as the subject should be in the *nominative case*.

I am younger than **he** (is young). (*he*—subject)
John can run as fast as **we** (can run). (*we*—subject)

In the unfinished clause of comparison the word *than* is a conjunction, and not a preposition. The word *than* introduces a clause which must be finished grammatically. When we supply the words that are necessary to complete the clause, we realize that the form of the pronoun should be *he* and not *him*. *He* is the correct form to use for the subject. The subject requires the *nominative case*.

Study the following illustrations carefully. Pay special attention to the form of the pronoun used in the *adverbial clause of comparison*.

You have lived longer than *I* (have lived). (not *me*)
Martha sews as well as *she* (sews). (not *her*)
Some of the men worked harder than *we* (worked). (not *us*)
I speak as correctly as *he* (does). (not *him*)

"As—As" and "Not So—As"
In Comparisons

The connectives *as—as* and *not so—as* are often used in sentences that contain adverbial clauses of comparison. Careful writers and speakers make a distinction in the use of these combinations. They use *as—as* when the comparison is **positive**, and *not so — as* when the comparison is **negative.**

The comparison is said to be positive when the two things compared are approximately the same or equal. The comparison is said to be negative when there is an inequality between the two things compared. An illustration will help make this clear.

John is **as** tall **as** his brother. (positive comparison)
John is **not so** tall **as** his father. (negative comparison)

In the first sentence, the comparison is *positive*. The two persons compared are approximately *equal* in height. The combination *as—as* is used to indicate this type of comparison. In the second sentence, the combination *not so—as* is used to show an *inequality* in height, or a *negative* comparison.

In speaking and in informal writing *as—as* is commonly used to show both types of comparison—positive and negative. However, in formal writing it is advisable to observe the distinctions that discriminating writers make.

Use of "Like" in Clauses

The word *like* is commonly used as a preposition. When the word *like* is used as a preposition, it should be followed by an object. If the object is a pronoun, the pronoun should be in the *objective case*. This usage was explained in Chapter 16.

Many careful speakers and writers feel that *like* should not be used as a conjunction to introduce a subordinate clause of manner or comparison. The words *as, as if,* and *as though* should be used to introduce this type of clause.

I shall write the letter *like* you advised me. (colloquial)
I shall write the letter *as* you advised me. (preferred)

You look *like* you were tired. (colloquial)
You look *as if* you were tired. (preferred)

185

It looks *like* it might snow. (colloquial)
It looks *as if* it might snow. (preferred)

In the last few years, the colloquial use of *like* as a conjunction has increased. This use sometimes appears in print. We often hear the word *like* used as a conjunction in popular television programs. However, in general, it has not been accepted as standard English for written use.

When *like* is used as a preposition, it means *similar to*, or *in a similar manner to*.

Mary's hat is *like* the one I bought in Paris. (*like*—preposition)
John is *like* his father in temperament. (*like*—preposition)

20. NOUN CLAUSES

Chapters Eighteen and Nineteen explained the form and function of two types of subordinate clause—the *adjective clause* and the *adverbial clause*. In this unit you will study the form and function of another type of subordinate clause—the *noun clause*.

You have learned that adjective clauses and adverbial clauses are used as *modifiers* in the same way that adjectives and adverbs are used as modifiers. Noun clauses are not used as modifiers. They perform the same functions that a *noun* performs.

FUNCTION OF THE NOUN CLAUSE
Noun Clause—Subject of a Sentence

A noun is commonly used as the *subject* of a sentence. A *noun clause* may also be used as the **subject** of a sentence. The following illustrations show how the noun clause is used as the subject of a sentence. The whole clause is the subject.

<u>What the chairman proposed</u> was not practical.
<u>How you manage on your income</u> is a puzzle to me.
<u>That their house is for sale</u> is a well-known fact.
<u>Where we could find an apartment</u> was our problem.

The subject of a sentence usually tells what we are talking about. The noun clause in the first sentence tells *what* was not practical; namely, *What the chairman proposed*. In the second sentence, the subject, or the noun clause, tells *what* it is that is a puzzle to me; namely, *How you manage on your income*. In the third sentence, the noun clause tells *what* is a well-known fact; namely, *That their house is for sale*. The noun clause in the last sentence tells *what our problem was*.

If you examine the preceding illustrations, you will see that the following words introduce the noun clauses: *what, how, that*, and *where*. These same words are often used to introduce adjective or adverbial clauses. The only way to be sure that you are dealing with a *noun clause* is to determine how the clause is used in the sentence. If it functions in the way that a noun functions, it is a noun clause.

Noun Clause—Direct Object of a Verb

A *noun clause* is frequently used as the **direct object** of a verb. A noun used as an object completes the meaning of the verb and answers the question *What?* A noun clause used as the direct object of a verb completes the verb and in almost all cases answers the question *What?* Study the following illustrations. They show how noun clauses are used as objects of verbs:

I hope (*what?*) that you will be promoted. (object of *hope*)

We knew (*what?*) where we could park the car. (object of *knew*)

Tell the manager (*what?*) why you are leaving. (object of *tell*)

I believe (*what?*) that it is going to rain. (object of *believe*)

He understood (*what?*) what we were trying to do. (object of *understood*)

The noun clause in the first sentence tells *what I hope*. It is used as the object of the verb *hope*. The noun clause in the second sentence tells *what we knew*. It is the object of the verb *knew*. The noun clause in the third sentence tells *what you should tell the manager*. It is the object of the verb *tell*. The noun clause in the fourth sentence tells *what I believe*. The noun clause in the last sentence tells *what he understood*.

Noun Clause—Predicate Noun

A *noun clause* may be used as a **predicate noun** after one of the linking verbs. Like the predicate noun, a noun clause used after a linking verb means the same as the subject. It is also used to complete the verb. The noun clauses in the following sentences are used as *predicate nouns* after linking verbs:

The rumor was <u>that he had left the city.</u> (means the same as *rumor*)

That is <u>what we agreed to do.</u> (means the same as *that*)

My first impression was <u>that I had seen him before.</u> (means the same as *impression*)

The report was <u>that he was drowned.</u> (means the same as *report*)

The noun clause in the first sentence is *that he had left the city*. It completes the verb *was* and means the same as the subject *rumor*. The noun clause in the second sentence is *what we agreed to do*. It completes the linking verb *is* and means the same as the subject *that*. The noun clause in the third sentence is *that I had seen him before*. It completes the linking verb *was* and means the same as the subject *impression*. The noun clause in the last sentence means the same as *report* and completes the linking verb *was*.

Noun Clause—Object of a Preposition

Like the noun, a *noun clause* is sometimes used as the **object of a preposition.** You may often find it difficult to determine whether the noun clause is the object of the preposition or whether some word in the clause is the object of the preposition. If you study the following illustrations carefully, you will see why an entire *clause* is the object of the preposition.

Give the message to <u>whoever is in the office.</u> (noun clause—object of the preposition *to*)

We did not agree about <u>what the doctor ordered.</u> (noun clause—object of the preposition *about*)

Do the job in <u>whatever way you wish.</u> (noun clause—object of *in*)

In the first sentence, the noun clause *whoever is in the office* is the object of the preposition *to. Whoever* could not be the object of the preposition because it is the subject of the clause. In addition, the sentence does not mean that you should give the message to *whoever*. It means that you should give the message to *whoever is in the office*. The entire clause is the object of the preposition *to*.

In the second sentence, the noun clause *what the doctor ordered* is the object of the preposition *about*. The sentence does not mean that we did not agree about *what*. It means that we did not agree about *what the doctor ordered*. The word *what* could not be the object of the preposition because it has another function to perform in the clause. It is the object of the verb *ordered*.

The noun clause in the third sentence must be the object of the preposition. The word *way* could not be the object of the preposition because that is not the meaning intended. The sentence does not mean that you should do the job in *whatever way*, but it means that you should do the job in *whatever way you wish*. The entire clause is the object of the preposition *in*.

OMISSION OF THE CONNECTING WORD

Sometimes the word that introduces a subordinate clause is omitted. The reason for this omission is to bring the main idea and the subordinate idea closer together. Although the best writers and speakers often omit the connecting word, you should supply it whenever there is any doubt about the construction of the clause.

I believe <u>that</u> you will be promoted. (*that*—subordinate conjunction)

I believe you will be promoted. (subordinate conjunction omitted)

NOUN CLAUSE USED AS AN APPOSITIVE

A noun is often used *in apposition* with another noun. The word **apposition** comes from two Latin words which mean "*placed by*" or "*put near to*." A word in *apposition* is placed near another word to explain it or to identify it in some way. We often speak of a person and then add something to explain who the person is, or to identify him in some way.

Mike, our *janitor*, is very accommodating.
We called on Dr. Allen, a famous *scientist*.
Paris, a *city* in France, is famous as a fashion center.

In the first sentence, the noun *janitor* is in apposition with the noun *Mike*. It explains who Mike was. In the second sentence, *scientist* is in apposition with *Dr. Allen*. It identifies him as a scientist. In the third sentence, *city* is in apposition with *Paris*.

In all three sentences the nouns that are in apposition with other nouns are set off by commas. Sometimes the appositive is so closely connected with the noun that no commas are required. It is not good practice to set off the appositive by commas in sentences like the following:

My brother Andrew is in London.
The poet Whittier wrote "Snowbound."

Like the noun, a *noun clause* is often used in **apposition** with a word or a group of words. When the noun clause is used in apposition, it usually explains such words as *idea, fact, belief, report, rumor*, etc. Noun clauses used in apposition are not set of by commas.

The rumor that John would be elected spread rapidly.
The fact that the contract was signed was important.

191

The announcement that the strike was over was received with cheers.

We entertained the hope that the crew had survived.

NOUN CLAUSE AND THE INTRODUCTORY "IT"

Sometimes a sentence begins with the introductory word *it*. In sentences of this type the word *it* is not the real subject of the sentence. The grammatical or real subject appears later. The real subject is often a *noun clause.* Sentences are arranged in this way either for emphasis or for smoothness.

It is obvious that you do not have the money.

(It) That you do not have the money is obvious. (*transposed order*)

This sentence begins with the introductory word *it*. The real or grammatical subject appears later in the sentence. The subject is the noun clause, *that you do not have the money.* When the sentence was transposed, the word *it*, which has no grammatical connection with any part of the sentence, was dropped, and the real subject was put in its proper place.

The word *it* has only one purpose in sentences of this type. It fills in the place normally occupied by the subject. Its function is similar to that of the introductory word *there*, which was explained in Chapter Four. When the word *it* is used in this way, it is called an **expletive.**

Sentences that begin with *it* as an expletive, or "filling in" word, are easily recognized because they always follow the same pattern:

It is important that you see him at once.

(It) That you see him at once is important. (*transposed order*)

WORDS THAT INTRODUCE
NOUN CLAUSES

A *noun clause* may be introduced by a **subordinate conjunction.** The subordinate conjunctions commonly used in this way are *that, whether*, and *whether or*. The sole duty of the subordinate conjunction is to connect the noun clause to the main clause.

I wonder *whether* they will recognize me.
John knows *that* he will be nominated for an office.

Whether (not *if*) should be used to introduce noun clauses used as the direct object of the verbs *say, learn, understand, know, doubt, ask, tell, discover, wonder*, etc.

Ask John *if* he has washed the car. (incorrect)
Ask John *whether* he has washed the car. (correct)

I did not know *if* he would leave or stay. (incorrect)
I did not know *whether* he would leave or stay. (correct)

A noun clause is often introduced by a **relative pronoun:** *who, what, whatever, whoever, whomever, whichever. Whoever* and *whomever* are seldom used in informal writing and speaking.

The agent does not know *what* he should do about repairs.
Give to the fund *whatever* you can afford.
A copy of the speech was given to *whoever* wanted it.

The relative pronoun that introduces a noun clause is sometimes called an **indefinite relative pronoun** because it does not have an antecedent expressed in the sentence.

Sometimes the relative pronoun is used as an *adjective* in the noun clause. A pronoun used in this way is called a **relative adjective,** or an **indefinite relative adjective** because it has no antecedent.

I shall accept *whatever salary* is offered me. (*whatever*—adjective modifies *salary*)

The manager always knows *what course* he should follow. (*what*—adjective modifies *course*)

Noun clauses are also introduced by the adverbs *how, when, why,* and *where.* The introductory adverb also modifies the verb in the noun clause. The noun clause is underlined in the following sentences.

How we should invest the money is the question. (*how*—adverb)

He asked where the president lived. (*where*—adverb)

I do not know when the speaker will arrive. (*when*—adverb)

21. PARTICIPLES

THE NATURE OF VERBALS

There are three verb forms in English that are known as **verbals:** *participles, gerunds,* and *infinitives.* Participles are discussed in this unit, gerunds in Chapter 22, and infinitives in Chapter 23. These verb forms are called *verbals* because they are derived from verbs and retain many of the characteristics of the verb.

A **verbal** may take any kind of modifier or any kind of complement that a verb might take. In addition to this verb-like function, a verbal has a special function of its own. A verbal usually performs the work of two parts of speech at the same time.

There is one function that a *verbal* cannot perform. It cannot function as the predicate verb in a sentence because it is an incomplete form of the verb. A verbal cannot make a statement or ask a question.

A **participle** is a verbal (verb form) which is *used as an adjective.* Since a participle is a verb form and partakes of the nature of a verb, it may take modifiers and complements.

Participles do not always take modifiers or complements. Very often they are used as **pure adjectives** and are placed directly before the nouns which they modify. Sometimes they are used as **predicate adjectives** after linking verbs. The following illustrations show the participle used as a simple adjective:

He conducts a *flourishing* business. (*flourishing* — modifies *business*)

The reports were *discouraging.* (*discouraging*—modifies *reports*)

We are reading an *interesting* book. (*interesting*—modifies *book*)

The participle that is most commonly used as an adjective is the participle that ends in *ing*. This is called the **present participle.** In the following illustrations the *present participles* are placed directly before the nouns which they modify. When used in this way, they are generally regarded as pure adjectives.

running water	*singing* brook
shaking knees	*rustling* leaves
murmuring pines	*dangling* modifiers
coming events	*whistling* boy
soaring prices	*sleeping* child

The participles found in the preceding illustrations are *running*, *shaking*, *murmuring*, *coming*, *soaring*, *singing*, *rustling*, *dangling*, *whistling*, and *sleeping*. All these forms are derived from verbs.

Many participles are used as pure adjectives. When the participle is used as a pure adjective, it is usually placed directly before the noun which it modifies. When the participle is used as a **predicate adjective,** it is found in the predicate and modifies the subject.

The game was *exciting*. (*exciting*—used as a predicate adjective)

The book is *interesting*. (*interesting*—predicate adjective)

The rumors were *startling*. (*startling*—used as a predicate adjective)

In the first sentence, the participle *exciting* is used as a predicate adjective, modifying the noun *game*. The participle *interesting*, in the second sentence, modifies the noun *book*. In the third sentence, the participle *startling* is used as a predicate adjective, modifying the subject noun *rumors*. The participles *exciting*, *interesting*, and *startling* are forms of verbs.

FORMS OF THE PARTICIPLE

There are three participles that are commonly used as adjectives: the *present participle* (active voice); the *past participle* (passive voice); and the *perfect participle* (active voice). There is no active past participle in English.

These participles are easily recognized. The **present participle** always ends in *ing;* the **past participle** usually ends in *ed, d, t, n,* or *en.* The past participles of some of the irregular verbs do not have distinctive endings: *swum, drunk, gone, sung,* etc. The **perfect participle** is always formed by prefixing the word *having* to the past participle: *having sung, having called, having driven, having seen,* etc.

Regular Verbs

Present Participle (*active*)	Past Participle (*passive*)	Perfect Participle (*active*)
calling	called	having called
watching	watched	having watched

Irregular Verbs

singing	sung	having sung
driving	driven	having driven
going	gone	having gone

PAST PARTICIPLES AND PERFECT PARTICIPLES

The past participle ending in *ed* is commonly used as an adjective. The following illustrations show how *past participles* function as *adjectives*:

A doctor, **called** to the scene, examined the injured man.

The **neglected** and **forgotten** child was picked up by an officer.

The army, **surprised** by the attack, fled into the woods.

The street was littered with paper, **thrown** from the windows.

In the first sentence, the past participle, *called* is used as an adjective to modify *doctor*. The participle is modified by the adverbial phrase, *to the scene*. There are two past participles in the second sentence, *neglected* and *forgotten*. One ends in *ed* and the other ends in *en*. These participles modify the noun *child*. In this sentence, the participles are placed directly before the noun *child*, which they modify.

The past participle *surprised* in the third sentence modifies *army*. The participle is modified by the adverbial phrase *by the attack*. The past participle *thrown* in the last sentence is modified by the adverbial phrase *from the windows*. The participle *thrown* modifies the noun *paper*.

The following sentences show the adjective use of the *perfect participle*:

Having finished the dress, Mary packed it carefully in a box.
Having completed the job, the men left early.
Having accomplished his mission, the ambassador returned home.
Having recovered completely, Ted left the hospital.

The perfect participles in the preceding illustrations are *having finished, having completed, having accomplished*, and *having recovered*. The first three take direct objects—*dress, job*, and *mission*. The last one, *having recovered*, is modified by the adverb *completely*. They are all in the active voice.

The perfect participle, *having finished*, modifies the noun *Mary*. *Having completed* modifies the noun *men; having accomplished* modifies *ambassador*, and *having recovered* modifies *Ted*. These participles are used as adjectives.

THE PARTICIPIAL PHRASE

Since the participle is derived from a verb, it retains many of the characteristics of a verb. Like the verb, a participle may take **modifiers** and **complements.** The participle with its *modifiers* or *complements*, or with both complements and modifiers is called a **participial phrase.**

MODIFIERS OF PARTICIPLES

A participle is often modified by an adverb or an adverbial phrase:

Looking up suddenly, Robert saw a rainbow in the sky.
Coming close to the rock, we saw a strange sight.

In the first sentence, the participle *looking* modifies the noun *Robert*. The participle *looking* is modified by the adverb *up* and the adverb *suddenly*. *Looking up suddenly* is a **participial phrase.**

In the second sentence, the participle *coming* modifies the pronoun *we*. The participle *coming* is modified by the adverb *close* and the adverbial phrase *to the rock*. *Coming close to the rock* is a **participial phrase.**

The participles in the following sentences also take *adverbial modifiers*:

Trembling with excitement, Sara waited for her friends.
(Participial phrase modifies the noun *Sara*.)
The house, remodeled recently, is very attractive.
(Participial phrase modifies the noun *house*.)
We saw an old man lying on the road.
(Participial phrase modifies the noun *man*.)

In the first sentence, the participial phrase consists of the participle *trembling* and its modifier, the adverbial phrase *with excitement*. The phrase, taken as a whole, modifies the noun *Sara*. The participial phrase *trembling with excitement* is used as an adjective, modifying *Sara*.

In the second sentence, the participial phrase consists of the participle *remodeled* and the adverbial modifier, the adverb

199

recently. The entire phrase, *remodeled recently*, is used as an adjective, modifying the noun *house*.

In the third sentence, the participial phrase is *lying on the road*. It consists of the participle *lying* and the adverbial phrase *on the road*. The entire phrase, *lying on the road*, modifies the noun *man*.

COMPLEMENTS OF PARTICIPLES

1. Like the verb, a participle may take a direct object if the verb expresses action.

<u>Carrying</u> a <u>suitcase</u>, the porter entered the train.
<u>Realizing</u> the <u>danger</u>, the captain ordered a retreat.

In the first sentence, the noun *suitcase* is the direct object of the participle *Carrying*. The entire expression, *Carrying a suitcase*, is a participial phrase. The participial phrase modifies the noun *porter*.

In the second sentence, the noun *danger* is the direct object of the participle *realizing*. The entire expression, *Realizing the danger*, is a participial phrase. The participial phrase modifies the noun *captain*.

2. Like the verb, a participle may be followed by a predicate noun or a predicate adjective.

Participles that take predicate nouns or predicate adjectives as complements are forms of *linking verbs*.

<u>Being</u> an <u>invalid</u>, he could not climb the steep hill.
<u>Becoming weary</u>, the traveler sat down to rest.

In the first sentence, the participle *being* is followed by the predicate noun *invalid*. The noun *invalid* refers to the same person as the subject *he*. The entire expression, *being an invalid*, is a participial phrase. The participial phrase modifies the subject pronoun *he*. *Being* is a form of the linking verb *to be*.

In the second sentence, the participle *becoming* is followed by the predicate adjective *weary*. The entire expression, *becoming weary*, is a participial phrase, modifying the noun *traveler*. *Becoming* is a form of the linking verb *to become*.

PARTICIPLES USED IN INDEPENDENT CONSTRUCTIONS

Sometimes a participle is used with a noun in an independent construction; that is, the participle and the noun which it modifies are not related grammatically to any other part of the sentence. Such a construction is called the **nominative absolute construction.**

The term *absolute* is used because the entire expression is an *independent construction*. It forms part of a sentence, but is not connected with the rest of the sentence grammatically. The term *nominative* is used because the noun which the participle modifies is in the *nominative case*. The following illustrations will make this use of the participle clear. The independent constructions are underlined.

The sun having set, we decided to return home.
The train being late, the soldiers missed the boat.

In the first sentence, the expression, *The sun having set*, consists of the perfect participle *having set* and the noun *sun* with its modifier *The*. The entire expression, *The sun having set*, is used *absolutely* or independently. It has no grammatical connection with the rest of the sentence. The noun *sun* is in the nominative case.

The expression, *The train being late*, in the second sentence is also a *nominative absolute construction*; that is, it has no grammatical relation to the rest of the sentence. The noun *train* is in the nominative case. It is modified by the expression *being late*, which consists of the participle *being* and the predicate adjective *late*.

DANGLING PARTICIPLES

Participles are often used incorrectly in speaking and writing. One of the most common mistakes in English is to use what is commonly referred to as the **dangling participle.** Anything that dangles is said *to hang loosely*, without secure attachment. A participle ''dangles'' when there is no word in the sentence which it could properly modify, or when it seems to be related to a word which does not convey the meaning intended.

It is easy to detect these loose participial modifiers. Sometimes the use of a *dangling modifier* gives a ridiculous or a humorous slant to the meaning of the sentence. You can avoid this error if you think through your sentences carefully and relate the participle to the proper word.

When the participial phrase is placed at the beginning of a sentence, it should refer to the subject. When it could not possibly modify the subject from the standpoint of meaning, the sentence must be rewritten and a suitable subject supplied which it could logically modify.

Walking through the tunnel, a wallet was picked up.
Entering the harbor, the Statue of Liberty came into view.
Taking the test, the teacher gave me a passing grade.

In the first sentence, the participial phrase *walking through the tunnel* modifies the subject of the sentence, which is *wallet*. A participle used at the beginning of a sentence modifies the subject. It is evident that the wallet was not walking through the tunnel; however, that is the meaning conveyed by the sentence as it is written. Very often the best way to get rid of a dangling participle is to substitute a clause for it.

While we were walking through the tunnel, we picked up a wallet.

In the second sentence, the participial phrase modifies *Statue of Liberty*. But it was not the *Statue of Liberty* that was entering

202

the harbor. The ph se seems to be related to a word which it could not modify. The word which the participial phrase really modifies is not in the sentence. The sentence might be revised as follows:

As we entered the harbor, the Statue of Liberty came into view.

In the last sentence, the participial phrase modifies the word *teacher*. If you read the sentence carefully, you will readily see that it was not the teacher who took the test. The sentence would be correctly written if a clause were substituted for the dangling phrase.

After I took the test, the teacher gave me a passing grade.

MISPLACED MODIFIERS

Sometimes there is a word in the sentence which the participial phrase properly modifies, but the participle is not placed correctly. As a result, the meaning is confused. This error is commonly referred to as a **misplaced modifier.**

Jumping into the water, the children were rescued by the life guard.
Several soldiers passed by in their uniforms recently drafted.

If you read the first sentence carefully, you will see that the word which the participle modifies is in the sentence. It is the word *lifeguard*. It was the *lifeguard* who jumped into the water. It was not the *children*. The trouble with the sentence is that the participial phrase should modify the subject. As the sentence is written, the subject is *children*. The subject should be the word *lifeguard*. The sentence might be rewritten as follows:

Jumping into the water, the lifeguard rescued the children.

In the second sentence, a participial modifier is also misplaced. As the sentence is written, the participial phrase modifies the word *uniforms*. But it was not the *uniforms* that were recently drafted; it was the *soldiers*. The sentence might be rewritten as follows:

Several recently drafted soldiers passed by in their uniforms.

PARTICIPLES USED IN VERB PHRASES

Participles are not always used as adjectives. One of their most important uses is to help form a *verb phrase*. When the participle forms part of a verb phrase, it is not considered as a separate word, but as part of the verb phrase.

A participle is never used alone as the predicate verb in a sentence because it is an incomplete form of the verb. It is used as part of a verb phrase. The following illustrations show how the participle is used as part of a verb phrase:

The janitor <u>is washing</u> the windows. (*washing*—part of verb phrase)

The gardener <u>has planted</u> the shrubs. (*planted*—part of verb phrase)

In the first sentence, the verb phrase *is washing* is made up of the auxiliary verb is and the present participle of the verb *wash*, or the *ing* participle, *washing*. In the second sentence, the verb phrase *has planted* is made up of the auxiliary *has* and the past participle of the verb *plant*, which is *planted*.

Sometimes it is difficult to determine whether the participle is part of the verb phrase, or whether it is used as an adjective modifying the subject. This is often true when a participle follows a linking verb. The meaning of the sentence will help you determine which use is intended by the speaker or writer. Study the following sentences carefully:

The talk was *inspiring*. (participle, used as an *adjective*)
We *were inspired* by his talk. (participle, part of *verb phrase*)

In the first sentence, the verb is *was*, not *was inspiring*. The verb *was* is a linking verb and requires a complement. In this sentence the complement is *inspiring*, which is used as a predicate adjective modifying the noun *talk*. The sentence means *inspiring talk*. *Inspiring* is a participle used as an adjective.

In the second sentence, the verb is *were inspired*. In this sentence, the past participle *inspired* is part of the verb phrase, *were inspired*. Study the following sentences carefully. Try to determine whether the participle is used as an adjective or is part of the verb phrase:

Robert <u>was elected</u> secretary at our last meeting. (*elected*— part of the verb phrase)

The old man looked <u>neglected</u>. (*neglected*—participle used as adjective)

The milk seems <u>frozen</u>. (*frozen*—participle used as adjective)

The house <u>was furnished</u> by an interior decorator. (*furnished*— part of verb phrase)

I <u>have been sitting</u> here for an hour. (*sitting*—part of verb phrase)

22. GERUNDS

Nature of the Gerund

If you understand the dual nature of the participle, you will have little difficulty in understanding the dual nature of the **gerund.** You have already learned that the participle is both *verb* and *adjective*. The gerund is both *verb* and *noun*.

Gerunds are like participles in many respects. Gerunds and participles are verbals; that is, they are *forms derived from verbs.* Both participles and gerunds have the same "*ing*' forms. Both take the same kinds of complements and modifiars that verbs take.

Gerunds differ from participles in one fundamental respect. **Gerunds** *are verb forms used as nouns*. Participles are verb forms used as adjectives. Because a gerund functions as a noun, it can take certain modifiers that a participle cannot take. Like the noun, a gerund is often modified by an *adjective* or by an *adjective phrase*. Participles cannot take adjective modifiers.

Since the gerund functions as a noun, it may be used as the *subject* of a sentence, the *direct object* of a verb, the *object of a preposition,* or as a *predicate noun* after one of the linking verbs. Gerunds are often called *verbal nouns* because they are derived from verbs.

Painting is Martha's hobby. (gerund used as *subject).*

Martha enjoys painting. (gerund used as *direct object)*

Martha earns a living by painting. (gerund used as *object of a preposition)*

Martha's hobby is painting. (gerund used as a *predicate noun)*

In the first sentence, the word *painting* is a gerund. It is a verb form that is used as a noun. *Painting* is the subject of the sentence. In the second sentence the same verb form *painting* is used as the direct object of the verb *enjoys*. . In the third sentence *painting* is used as the object of the preposition *by*, and in the fourth sentence it is used as a predicate noun after the linking verb *is*.

The Gerund Phrase

Like the participle, the gerund retains many of the characteristics of a verb. Because the gerund is a verb form, it may take any of the complements or any of the modifiers that a verb might take. The gerund with its complements and modifiers is called a **gerund phrase.**

COMPLEMENTS OF GERUNDS

Like the verb, a *gerund* may take a **direct object.** Study the following sentence carefully. You will readily see that although the gerund is used as a noun, it retains the characteristics of a verb because it takes a *direct object*.

Sweeping the floor was one of Jack's duties.

In this sentence the *sweeping* is a gerund. It is used as the *subject* of the sentence. This is its noun function. Since the gerund is a verb form. it retains some of the characteristics of a verb. The verb *sweep* is an action verb and may take a *direct object*. The gerund *sweeping* may also take a direct object. In this sentence the direct object of the gerund *sweeping* is the noun *floor*.

Some verbs take both a direct and an indirect object. Gerunds formed from such verbs may also take a **direct** and an **indirect object.**

Giving the girls a holiday will please them.

In this sentence, *giving* is a gerund used as the subject of the sentence. This is its use as a **noun.** As a **verb form,** it takes the direct object *holiday* and the indirect object *girls*. The entire expression, *giving the girls a holiday* is a **gerund phrase.**

If the gerund is a form of a linking verb, it may take a **predicate noun** or a **predicate adjective** as a *complement*.

Study the following sentences carefully. In both sentences the gerund requires a complement to complete its meaning. The gerunds are forms of linking verbs.

His <u>becoming a captain</u> involved certain responsibilities.
I had not heard of Jane's <u>being ill</u>.

In the first sentence, the gerund *becoming* takes the predicate noun *captain* as a complement. In the second sentence, the gerund *being* takes the predicate adjective *ill* as a complement.

ADVERBIAL MODIFIERS OF GERUNDS

The gerund, like the participle, may be modified by an **adverb** or an **adverbial phrase.** You should have no trouble in identifying the adverbial modifiers of the gerunds in the following sentences:

Sitting <u>on a park bench</u> was his favorite pastime.
Driving a truck <u>in the city</u> is difficult.
I do not advise your <u>seeing</u> him <u>now</u>.

The gerund *sitting* in the first sentence is modified by the adverbial phrase *on a park bench*. The gerund *driving* in the second sentence is modified by the adverbial phrase *in the city*. The gerund *seeing* in the third sentence is modified by the adverb *now*.

ADJECTIVE MODIFIERS OF GERUNDS

Because the gerund functions as a noun, it may be modified by an *adjective,* or by a *noun* or a *pronoun* used as an *adjective*.

The <u>slow driving</u> in the mountains irritated Max.
(*slow*—adjective, modifying the gerund *driving*)
The <u>dog's barking</u> saved the child's life.
(*dog's*—noun used as an adjective, modifying *barking*)
The critics praised her wonderful dancing.
(*her*—pronoun used as an adjective, modifying *dancing*)

(*wonderful*—adjective, modifying *dancing*)

In the first sentence, the gerund *driving* is modified by the adjective *slow*. In the second sentence, the gerund *barking* is modified by the word *dog's,* which is a noun in the possessive case used as an adjective. In the third sentence, the gerund *dancing* is modified by the possessive adjective *her* (pronoun used as an adjective) and the adjective *wonderful.*

Like the noun, a gerund is often modified by an *adjective phrase*. In the following sentences, the gerunds take adjective phrases as modifiers:

We heard the rustling of the leaves.
The villagers listened to the tolling of the bell.

In the first sentence, the gerund *rustling* is modified by the adjective phrase *of the leaves*. You can readily see that the adjective phrase modifies *rustling* because the sentence means that we heard the *leaves' rustling*.The second sentence means that the villagers listened to the *bell's tolling*.

THE POSSESSIVE CASE
BEFORE THE GERUND

The gerund is frequently modified by a noun or a pronoun in the *possessive case*. A mistake commonly made is to forget to put the noun or pronoun in the possessive case to show that it is a modifier. The important word in such sentences is the *gerund,* and not the modifier. The following illustration will help to make this clear:

The men objected to me playing on the team. (*incorrect*)

The men objected to my playing on the team. (*correct*)

The first sentence is incorrect because it conveys the wrong meaning. The sentence does not mean that the men objected to *me*. The word *me* is not the object of the preposition *to*.

The object of the preposition *to* is the gerund *playing*. The sentence means that the men objected to the *playing*. The use of the form *me* before the gerund is incorrect. The possessive form *my* should be used.

The following sentences are incorrect because the wrong form of the noun or pronoun is used before the gerund:

I am interested in <u>William advancing</u> in his profession (*incorrect*)

Mother did not like <u>me taking</u> part in the contest. (*incorrect*)

The first sentence does not mean that I am interested in *William* primarily. but that I am interested in *Williams's advancing*. The object of the preposition *in* is the gerund *advancing,* and not the proper noun *William*. Since the noun is a modifier of the gerund, it must be put in the possessive case (*William's* advancing).

The second sentence does not mean that Mother did not like *me*. It means that she *did* not like the *taking part in the contest*. The correct form of the pronoun before the gerund is *my* (*my* taking part).

THE DANGLING GERUND

Gerunds are often found in prepositional phrases which are placed at the beginning of the sentence. The gerund or the gerund phrase is the *object of the preposition*. The entire prepositional phrase should modify some word in the main part of the sentence. If there is no such word, the phrase "*dangles*" in the sentence; that is, the phrase is an unattached modifier.

The gerund almost always expresses action. There must be some word in the sentence to indicate the *doer* of this action. That word would logically be the subject of the sentence. Examine the following sentence carefully:

Upon receiving the telegram, the trip was cancelled.

This sentence begins with a prepositional phrase. The object of the preposition *upon* is the gerund phrase, *receiving the telegram*. The gerund *receiving* implies that someone received the telegram. The way the sentence is written, the *trip received the telegram*. The trouble with the sentence is that the subject has no logical relation to the gerund. The subject of the sentence should indicate *who* is doing the *receiving*. The following sentences are written correctly:

Upon <u>receiving</u> the telegram, *we* cancelled the trip.

   or

After <u>we had received</u> the telegram, we cancelled the trip.

This error might be corrected in one of two ways as shown in the preceding illustration:

1. By supplying the word which the prepositional phrase logically refers to.
2. By substituting a subordinate clause for the gerund phrase.

When the gerund phrase at the beginning of a sentence does not have a logical relation to the subject of the sentence, the result is often humorous. The careful study of a sentence like the following will help you understand the error and the reason for the correction:

By pressing a button, the table comes out of the wall. *(incorrect)* *(pressing—dangling gerund)*

This sentence clearly indicates that *someone must press a button* before *the table* will come out of the wall. According to the way in which the sentence is written, *the table* performs that function. Such an interpretation would be absurd.

The trouble with the sentence is that the *subject* has no logical relation to the *gerund*. The subject of the sentence should be a word that would indicate the *doer* of the action expressed by

211

the gerund. That word does not appear in the sentence as it is written. The sentence would be correctly written in either one of the following ways:

By pressing a button, <u>you will release</u> the table from the wall.

<u>If you press a button</u>, the table will come out of the wall.

23. INFINITIVES

Nature of the Infinitive

Participles, gerunds, and *infinitives* are called **verbals** because they are derived from verbs and function like verbs in many respects. They are unlike verbs because they cannot function as the predicate verb in a sentence. They are incomplete forms that cannot be used to make statements, ask questions, or give commands or requests. This is an important fact regarding verbals that you should always keep in mind.

You have learned how to recognize a participle or a gerund by its form. The infinitive is very easy to identify because it carries a definite sign which indicates that it is an infinitive. An infinitive is usually preceded by the word **to,** which is commonly called the *sign of the infinitive.*

When the word *to* is used with a verb form to complete the infinitive, it is *not a preposition.* It is merely the *sign* of the infinitive. The way to be sure that the expression is an infinitive, and not a prepositional phrase, is to look at the word which follows *to.* If this word is a verb form, the expression is an infinitive, and not a prepositional phrase.

Like the gerund, the infinitive is *used as a noun.* It may also function as an *adjective* or as an *adverb.* An infinitive may take any complement or any modifier that a verb might take.

The sign of the infinitive (*to*) is usually omitted after certain verbs in order to avoid awkward or stilted expressions. The *to* is usually omitted after the following verbs: *bear, feel, watch, let, dare, help, see, make, please, bid, need,* etc.

USES OF THE INFINITIVE

You have already studied the two-sided character of the participle and the gerund. The participle functions as an adjective and retains some of the characteristics of a verb. The gerund functions as a noun and also retains some of the characteristics of a verb. The **infinitive** retains its verb nature, and in addition may function as a *noun,* an *adjective,* or an *adverb.*

The noun function of an infinitive is very similar to the noun function of a gerund. An infinitive may be the *subject* of a sentence, the *direct object* of a verb, the *object of a preposition,* or a *predicate noun* after a linking verb.

To write was his ambition. *(subject)*

His ambition was to write. *(predicate noun)*

He did nothing except (to) write. *(object of preposition)*

He likes to write. *(direct object)*

In the first sentence, the infinitive *To write* is the subject of the sentence. In the second sentence, the infinitive *to write* is used as a predicate noun after the linking verb *was.* In the third sentence, the infinitive *to write* is used as the object of the preposition *except.* In this sentence, the sign of the infinitive is omitted. In the fourth sentence, the infinitive *to write* is used as the direct object of the verb *likes.*

INFINITIVES USED AS ADJECTIVES

The infinitive is often used as an *adjective* or an *adverb.* When the infinitive is used as an adjective, it usually modifies a noun which precedes it. It is easy to identify the adjective use of the infinitive because an adjective could be readily substituted for the infinitive. Study the following illustrations carefully:

The desire **to win** was apparent. *(the winning desire)*

They asked permission **to leave.** *(leaving permission)*

He obtained a permit **to build.** *(building permit)*

We had fresh water **to drink.** *(drinking water)*

In the first sentence, the infinitive *to win* is used as an adjective. It modifies the noun *desire.* In the second sentence, the infinitive *to leave* modifies the noun *permission*. In the third sentence, the infinitive *to build* modifies the noun *permit*. In the last sentence, the infinitive *to drink* modifies water.

INFINITIVES USED AS ADVERBS

The infinitive is often used as an *adverb* to modify a verb, an adjective, or an adverb. When the infinitive is used as an adverb, it usually expresses *purpose* or *degree*.

It is easy to identify an infinitive used as an adverb when it modifies a verb. In almost every case, the infinitive expresses *purpose*. It tells why, or for what purpose the action is performed. When an infinitive is used in this way, it is often called the *infinitive of purpose*. The infinitives in the following illustrations express purpose and modify the verb:

The traveler stopped **to rest.** *(to rest*—expresses purpose)
The composer came **to listen.** *(to listen*—expresses purpose)
The officer returned **to help.** (to help—expresses purpose)

In the first sentence, the infinitive *to rest* modifies the verb *stopped*. The infinitive expresses purpose; that is, it tells why the traveler stopped. The infinitive *to listen* modifies the verb *came*. The infinitive also expresses purpose. It tells why the composer came. The infinitive in the third sentence tells why the officer returned. It modifies the verb and expresses purpose.

An infinitive used as an adverb frequently modifies an *adjective*. This use of the infinitive is also easy to identify. In most cases, the infinitive modifies an adjective which follows a linking verb. Examine the following illustrations carefully:

The cake was ready **to bake.** *(to bake* modifies the adjective *ready)*
The men were anxious **to work.** *(to work* modifies the adjective *anxious)*
We are sorry **to leave.** *(to leave* modifies the adjective *sorry)*
I shall be glad **to help.** *(to help* modifies the adjective *glad)*

In the first sentence, the linking verb *was* is followed by the predicate adjective *ready*. The adjective *ready* is modified by the infinitive *to bake* which is used as an adverb. As you have learned, only adverbs can modify adjectives. The sentence means that the cake was ready *for baking*. The infinitive *to bake* could readily be turned into an adverbial phrase. This should make its adverbial function clear.

In the second sentence, the linking verb *were* is followed by the predicate adjective *anxious*. The adjective *anxious* is modified by the infinitive *to work*. In the third sentence, the predicate adjective *sorry* is modified by the infinitive *to leave*. In the last sentence, the predicate adjective *glad* is modified by the infinitive *to help*.

In all of the preceding illustrations a linking verb is followed by a predicate adjective. The predicate adjective is modified by an infinitive which is used as an adverb.

COMPLEMENTS OF INFINITIVES

Like the gerund and the participle, the infinitive may take any kind of complement a verb might take. Sometimes the infinitive takes a *direct object*. Sometimes it takes both a *direct* and an *indirect object*. If the infinitive is a form of a linking verb, it may take a *predicate noun* or a *predicate adjective* as a complement.

Arlene wanted to buy a fur coat. (*coat* object of *to buy*)

The tailor promised to make me a suit. (*me* indirect object) (*suit* direct object)

John would like to be an aviator. (*aviator* predicate noun)

His ambition is to become rich. (*rich* predicate adjective)

In the first sentence, the infinitive *to buy* takes the direct object *coat*. In the second sentence, the infinitive *to make* takes both an indirect object and a direct object. *Me* is the indirect object and *suit* is the direct object. In the third sentence, the infinitive *to be* takes the predicate noun *aviator* as a complement. In the last sentence, the infinitive *to become* takes the predicate adjective *rich* as a complement.

MODIFIERS OF INFINITIVES

1.   Like the verb, an infinitive may be modified by an *adverb* or by an *adverbial phrase*.

The boys like to swim <u>fast</u>. (*fast* adverb, modifies *to swim*)
The boys like to swim <u>in Lake Michigan</u>. (adverbial phrase modifies *to swim*)
To write <u>well</u> is an accomplishment. (*well* adverb modifies *To write*)
To fish <u>in that stream</u> is a pleasure. (adverbial phrase modifies *To fish*)

2.   Sometimes the infinitive has both a complement and a modifier.

To do the <u>job properly</u> would require a month's time.

In this sentence the infinitive *To do takes* the direct object *job*. The infinitive is also modified by the adverb *properly*.

THE INFINITIVE PHRASE

In the preceding illustration, the entire phrase, *To do the job properly*, regarded as a whole, is the **complete subject** of the sentence. This group of words is called an **infinitive phrase**. An *infinitive phrase* consists of an infinitive with its complements or its modifiers, or both if it takes both.

Ted's aim was <u>to please others</u>. (infinitive with a *direct object*)
We did not want <u>to travel by plane</u>. (infinitive with an *adverbial phrase* as a modifier)

The men would like to begin the project now. (infinitive with a *direct object* and an *adverb* as modifier)

The infinitive phrase in the first sentence is *to please others*. The phrase consists of the infinitive *to please* and its object *others*. The infinitive phrase in the second sentence is *to travel by plane*. It consists of the infinitive *to travel* and the adverbial phrase *by plane*, which modifies the infinitive. The infinitive phrase in the last sentence is *to begin the project now*. The infinitive takes the direct object *project* and the adverbial modifier *now*.

THE OMISSION OF THE SIGN 'TO'

You have learned that the sign of the infinitive (*to*) is omitted when the infinitive is used after certain verbs. The sign is not used because the sentence would sound awkward or stilted with the sign placed before the verb form. You should become familiar with the verbs that are followed by the infinitive without the sign "*to*."

The sign of the infinitive is usually omitted when the infinitive is used after the following verbs: *hear, feel let, watch, dare, help, see, make, please, bid, need, do*, etc. The following sentences illustrate the use of the infinitive without the sign. The *to* is enclosed in parentheses to show you that you should supply it mentally in order to recognize the infinitive construction.

1. I felt the floor (to) shake under me.
2. We heard him (to) sing some old ballads.
3. I saw her (to) enter the theater.
4. They bid us (to) leave immediately.
5. They dare not (to) create a disturbance.
6. Help me (to) carry the luggage.
7. Let his friend (to) help him.
8. They made him (to) wait for an hour.

24. PROBLEMS IN THE USE OF INFINITIVES

THE INFINITIVE CLAUSE

Sometimes the infinitive has its own *subject*. With this subject, the infinitive is used in a construction which is commonly called the **infinitive clause.** *The infinitive clause is not a true clause* because the infinitive cannot function as a predicate verb. An infinitive cannot function as the predicate verb in a clause because it is an incomplete verb form. The following illustrations will help make this clear:

The officers want the men to sing at the Rotary Club.
We believed him to be capable.

In the first sentence, the group of words, *the men to sing at the Rotary Club,* is called an **infinitive clause.** This expression is called a clause because the infinitive has a subject, and the entire group of words functions in the same way as a **noun clause** would function. The *infinitive clause* is used as the direct object of the verb *want.*

In the second sentence, the group of words *him to be capable* is an infinitive clause. The subject of the infinitive is the pronoun *him.* The entire expression *him to be capable* is used as the direct object of the verb *believed,* but it is not a true clause. The infinitive *to be* is not a predicate verb.

Jean asked me to go with her. (*me* subject of the infinitive *to go*)

Father advised him to buy the bonds. (*him* subject of the infinitive *to buy*)

He believed her to be honest. (*her* subject of the infinitive *to be*)

We want them to build a house. (*them* subject of the infinitive *to build*)

219

The underlined expression in each of the preceding sentences is the **object** of the preceding verb. In the first sentence, *me to go with her* is the object of the verb *asked*. The sentence does not mean that she asked *me*. It means that she asked *me to go with her*. The entire expression, *me to go with her,* is the object of the verb *asked*.

The group of words, *me to go with her,* is called an "infinitive clause." It consists of the subject *me* and the infinitive *to go* with the modifier of the infinitive, the adverbial phrase *with her*. You can readily see that this is not a true clause because the infinitive *to go* is an incomplete verb form and cannot function as the predicate verb.

The important fact to keep in mind about this construction is that the *subject* of the infinitive is always in the **objective case.** This is an *exception* to the rule that subjects of sentences and subjects of clauses are always in the nominative case.

Examine the preceding illustrations again. In the second sentence, *him* is the subject of the infinitive clause, *him to buy the bonds*. *Him* is in the objective case. In the third sentence, *her* is the subject of the infinitive clause, *her to be honest. Her* is in the objective case. In the last sentence, *them* is the subject of the infinitive clause *them to build a house. Them* is in the objective case.

You will not have any difficulty with the **case** of the subject of the infinitive. No one would think of saying, "Jean asked *I* to go with her," or "Father advised *he* to buy the bonds." It is natural to use the *objective case* as the subject of the infinitive. However, it is important to keep the following rule in mind. It will help you understand some of the other problems connected with the use of infinitives.

Sometimes the sign of the infinitive is omitted in the "infinitive clause." You must learn how to recognize such "clauses" even if the sign is omitted.

The manager made <u>Mary copy the report again.</u>

The manager made <u>Mary (to) copy the report again</u>.

I saw <u>her dance at the carnival</u>.
I saw <u>her (to) dance at the carnival</u>.

In the first sentence, the infinitive clause, *Mary (to) copy the report again*, is the direct object of the verb *made*. The sign of the infinitive *(to)* is omitted in this sentence. In the second sentence, the infinitive clause *her (to) dance at the carnival* is the object of the verb *saw*. The sign of the infinitive is omitted before *dance*.

VERB 'TO BE' IN AN INFINITIVE CLAUSE

When we use the infinitive *to be* in an "infinitive clause," we have a problem in agreement of subject and complement which is often confusing. You have just learned that the subject of an infinitive is always in the objective case. This rule applies in the case of *action verbs* and *linking verbs*.

The problem arises when the infinitive is a form of a linking verb. You learned in your previous study that the noun or pronoun used after a linking verb is in the *nominative case* to agree with the subject of the sentence. Up to this point, every word used as the subject of a sentence or of a clause has been in the nominative case. In the case of the "infinitive clause" we are dealing with a subject that is in the **objective case.**

The verb *to be*, as well as other linking verbs, always takes the same case after it as it takes before it. If the case before it is the *objective case*, the *objective case* must follow it. A noun or pronoun following a linking verb must be in the same case as the subject. Since the noun or pronoun that follows a linking verb means the same person or thing as the subject, it must agree with the subject in case. Therefore, the noun or pronoun that follows the verb *to be* in an infinitive clause is in the objective case to agree with the *subject*, which is in the objective case. This is the logical agreement of *subject* and *complement* after a linking verb functioning as an infinitive in an infinitive clause.

A few illustrations will make this clear. Notice the form of the pronoun after the linking verbs in the "infinitive clauses."

I should like the chairman to be him. *(chairman* objective case, *him* objective case)

Many of the guests thought us to be them. *(us* objective case, *them* objective case)

In the first sentence, the subject of the infinitive clause is *chairman*, which is in the objective case. The infinitive *to be* is followed by the predicate pronoun *him*. The pronoun used as the complement of a linking verb must agree in case with the subject. Since the subject is in the objective case, the pronoun must be in the objective case to agree with the subject.

In the second sentence, the pronoun *us* is the subject of the infinitive clause. *Us* is in the objective case. The pronoun that follows the infinitive *to be* must be in the same case as the subject. *Them* is in the objective case to agree with the case of the subject, *us*.

THE SPLIT INFINITIVE

The parts of an infinitive (*to* with a verb form) are regarded as a unit. They should not be separated unless there is a good reason for doing so. The usual method of separating the parts of the infinitive is to place an adverb between the *to* and the *verb form*. When the parts of the infinitive are separated in this way, we refer to the infinitive as a **"split infinitive."** The adverbial modifier "splits" the infinitive.

As a rule, the infinitive should *not* be split by a modifier. Sometimes it is both desirable and effective to split the infinitive, as many authorities in grammar are pointing out. Ordinarily, it is not the best practice, as you will readily see from the following illustrations:

I asked you **to** immediately **return** my camera.

The judge was determined **to** intently and carefully **examine** the evidence.

In the first sentence, the infinitive is *to return*. The adverbial modifier, *immediately,* is placed between the sign of the infinitive and the verb form. In this particular sentence there is no justifiable reason for splitting the infinitive. The sentence would sound much better if it were written as follows:

I asked you **to return** my camera immediately.

In the second sentence, two adverbial modifiers connected by *and* are placed between the parts of the infinitive. This sentence would sound better if the infinitive were not split in this matter.

The judge was determined **to examine** the evidence intently and carefully.

Many authorities in English call our attention to the fact that some of the best writers split infinitives. When writers do this, they have a good reason for the "split." They also know how to do it so that the sentence will not sound awkward or stilted. When a writer splits an infinitive, his purpose is to throw the emphasis in a certain direction. The following are examples of split infinitives found in good writing:

1. "I feel like inviting them to <u>first</u> consider"

2. "I desire to <u>so</u> arrange my affairs"

3. "his ability to <u>effectually</u> carry on"

4. "to <u>enable</u> him to properly perform his work"

5. "to <u>better</u> acquaint myself with the problems"

6. "Our object is to <u>further</u> cement trade relations."

7. "He worked silently and swiftly, hoping to <u>speedily</u> end his patient's discomfort."

Although there is plenty of evidence that good writers some-times split the infinitive, ordinarily it is better practice to keep the parts of the infinitive together. A writer or speaker should certainly avoid using such awkward sentences as the following:

Edwin was eager for me to <u>especially</u> see the art exhibit. (*to see* infinitive)

Eugene promised to <u>never again</u> be late to work. (*to be* infinitive)

The committee wanted to <u>beautifully</u> decorate the hall. (*to decorate* infinitive)

I want to <u>next year</u> go to Europe. *(to go* infinitive)

In the first sentence, the infinitive *to see* is "split" by placing the adverb *especially* between the sign of the infinitive *to* and the verb form *see*. In the second sentence, two adverbial mod-ifiers "split" the infinitive. In the third sentence, the adverb *beautifully* "splits" the infinitive. In the fourth sentence, the adverbial modifier *year* is placed between the sign *to* and the verb form, *go*. *Year* is a noun used as an adverb.

SPECIAL USES OF THE INFINITIVE

The infinitive is often used in **apposition** with a noun to explain or identify that noun. This is a very useful construction, for it enables us to explain the noun in a very few words. The infinitive used as an *appositive* is usually set off by commas. Sometimes a dash is used.

His first proposal, <u>to borrow money,</u> was rejected.
We were given our orders <u>to finish the job before ten.</u>

In the first sentence, the infinitive phrase, *to borrow money,* is in apposition with the word *proposal*. It explains the nature of the proposal or tells what the proposal was. In the second sentence, the infinitive phrase, *to finish the job before ten,* is in apposition with the word *orders*. It explains what our orders were.

The infinitive is also used as the **delayed subject** in a sentence that begins with the introductory word *it*. In this case *it* is an **expletive.**

It always pays <u>to tell the truth.</u>

(It) To tell the truth always pays.

It is your duty <u>to protect your interests.</u>

(It) To protect your interests is your duty.

Sentences that begin with the pronoun *it* used as an expletive should always be transposed in order to see the grammatical relations more clearly.

THE THREE SIDED CHARACTER OF THE INFINITIVE
Noun uses of the Infinitive

1. **Subject** of the sentence
2. **Direct object** of a verb
3. **Object** of a *preposition*
4. **Predicate noun** after a *linking verb*
5. **Appositive**
6. **Delayed subject** after an expletive
7. May take an *adjective modifier*

The Infinitive As A Modifier

1. May function as an **adjective,** modifying a noun
2. May function as an **adverb** expressing purpose or degree

Verb Characteristics Of The Infinitive

1. Expresses *action* or *state of being*, but *cannot* function as the predicate verb in a sentence
2. May take a complement: *direct object, indirect object, predicate noun,* or *predicate adjective*
3. May take modifier: *adverbs* and *adverbial phrases*
4. May form part of an infinitive clause.

25. PUNCTUATION REVIEW

All punctuation marks are "signals" from the writer to the reader. A period shows that a sentence has been ended or that an abbreviation has been used. A comma may show a slight break in thought, separate the two parts of a compound sentence, or be used in one of several other ways.

Keep in mind that *some sentences may be punctuated in more than one way* and that, in some instances, a punctuation mark may or may not be used at the writer's discretion.

Remember, also, that *some professions and businesses have their own style of punctuation*. A journalist, for example, may omit some punctuation marks which normally are included in a business letter. A lawyer, on the other hand, uses many more punctuation marks when preparing a legal form than are essential for most types of business writing.

OPEN AND CLOSED PUNCTUATION

The terms *open* and *closed* punctuation apply only to the business letter and only to the heading and inside address of the letter. They do not apply to the salutation and complimentary close. If your company uses *open* punctuation, as most firms do, *omit all commas and periods at the ends of lines in the heading and inside address* unless the line ends in an abbreviation. If your firm uses *closed* punctuation, *include commas and periods at the ends of the lines in the heading and in the inside address*. The following examples illustrate the two styles of punctuation. Remember that most firms prefer open punctuation.

Open Punctuation

Acme Rug Cleaners,
1823 Timber Avenue
New York, New York

Closed Punctuation

Acme Rug Cleaners
1823 Timber Avenue,
Mahwah, New Jersey.

226

The salutation and complimentary close of a business letter are usually punctuated by a colon after the salutation and a comma following the complimentary close, regardless of open or closed punctuation.

USE OF THE PERIOD

1. The period (.) is used after a declarative or an imperative sentence.

She went to the office. (declarative)

Close the car door. (imperative)

Exception: If you wish to give a declarative or an imperative sentence the force of an exclamatory sentence, use an exclamation point rather than a period.

I was so shocked that I was speechless! (declarative)

Bring the Pulmotor quickly! (imperative)

2. After requests, use a period rather than a question mark.

May I send you a copy of our latest bulletin. (request)

Will you send me any further information which you have available. (request)

3. The period is used after abbreviations and initials.

Dr.	Mrs.	A.M.	Jan.
Sr.	Sat.	C. I. Jones	Inc.
B.S.	Ph.D.	U.S.A.	Gen.

Note: When a sentence ends with an abbreviation, one period is sufficient for both the abbreviation and the sentence.

Mail the package to Conley and Green, Inc.

4. The period is used to indicate the omission of words in quoted passages.

(a) Use three periods (. . .) to indicate the omission of words within a quoted passage.

"I pledge allegiance to the flag of the United States. . . one nation, indivisible, with liberty and justice for all."

(b) Use four periods (. . . .) to indicate the omission of words at the end of a quoted passage.

"Fame is the spur . . . ." John Milton

USE OF THE COMMA

1. The comma (,) is used after an adverbial dependent clause when the dependent clause precedes the main clause. When

the dependent clause does not begin the sentence, the comma is usually unnecessary. (See Chapter 19 for a detailed discussion of adverbial clauses.)

<u>After the director had read the minutes of the meeting,</u> he called for the financial report. (comma)

The director called for the financial report <u>after he had read the minutes of the meeting.</u> (no comma)

    2. The comma is used after a participial phrase or an absolute phrase at the beginning of a sentence. (See Chapter 21 for a detailed discussion of participial phrases and absolute constructions.)

<u>Seeing the address across the street,</u> he wrote a note in his little book.

<u>The rain having stopped,</u> we went to lunch.

    3. The comma is used after an introductory infinitive phrase.

<u>To be successful,</u> you must read widely.

Note: When the subject of the sentence is an infinitive, do not separate the subject from the rest of the sentence.

<u>To be successful</u> was his goal.

    4. The comma is used to set off parenthetical expressions, whether words, phrases, or clauses.

(a) Transitional words such as *however, therefore, moreover, besides, consequently* should be set off by commas.

Consequently, I did not receive an answer to his letter.

Exception: The word *also* is not set off by commas unless the writer wishes *also* to be emphasized strongly. In such a case, *also* is generally placed in an unusual position in the sentence.

We also noticed that the salaries declined after the first of the year. (no emphasis).

Also, we noticed that the salaries declined after the first of the year (emphasis intended)

(b) Phrases such as *so to speak, in short, as a result, of course* should be set off by commas.

We found, in short, many errors in his work.
Of course, there are many ways to tackle the problem.

(c) Clauses such as *I think, we suppose, he says* should be set off by commas.

Someone, I suppose, should check the report.

(d) Explanatory expressions, such as *and I agree with him, so far as he is concerned,* etc., which break the logical sequence of words should be set off by commas.

The president disliked the policy, and I agreed with him, of letting all employees name their vacation time.

5. The comma is used after introductory expressions such as *yes, indeed, surely* (when it means *yes), well.*

Well, the next thing we knew he had shot the deer.
Yes, I will attend to the matter.

6. The comma is used to set off a nonrestrictive clause. A nonrestrictive clause is set off because *it is not essential to complete the meaning of a sentence.* A nonrestrictive clause is similar to a parenthetical expression in that it gives added information about the word it modifies.

Restrictive clauses are never set off by commas. *A restrictive clause is a clause that is necessary to complete the meaning of the sentence* because the clause identifies the word it modifies. A restrictive clause *cannot* be left out of a sentence, whereas a nonrestrictive clause can be. (See Chapter 18 for further information on restrictive and nonrestrictive clauses.)

The girl who lives next door came to work in our office. (The clause *who lives next door* is restrictive because it is needed to identify the word *girl*. The clause is not set off by commas.)

Mary Jones, who lives next door, came to work in our office. (The clause *who lives next door* is nonrestrictive because it is not needed to identify the name *Mary Jones*. The name *Mary Jones* clearly identifies the person being talked about, and the clause merely gives added information about the person *Mary Jones*.)

7. The comma is used to set off words in apposition. An appositive is a word or phrase that defines or identifies another word. An appositive means the same as the word it defines.

Jones, <u>our office manager</u>, is ill.

Reverend Brown, <u>our minister</u>, is an intelligent man.

Note 1: An appositive at the end of a sentence should be preceded by a comma.

I sent the memorandum to Jones, our office manager.

Note 2: Very closely related appositives do not require a comma.

my cousin Mary   Louis the Fourth
his friend Bill   Mary Queen of Scots

8. The comma is used to set off words used in direct address.

We regret, Mr. Thomas, that your order was unsatisfactorily filled.
Henry, bring me the December file.

9. The comma is used to separate a series of three or more words, phrases, or clauses.

Alice planned to have steak, potatoes, beans, lettuce, and ice cream for dinner.
He stalked off the stage, turned around, came back, and glared at the audience.

At the meeting it was decided to (1) give two weeks' vacation with pay, (2) give pensions at age sixty—five, (3) establish a profit sharing-plan.

Note 1: A comma should always be placed before the conjunction joining the last two members of a series.

She asked for paper, pencils, and a ruler.

Note 2: A comma should separate pairs of words in a series. A comma should not be placed before a conjunction joining words of a series that are considered as one unit.

Typing and shorthand, spelling and vocabulary, grammar and punctuation are the most popular courses. (pairs of words in a series)

For breakfast she ordered orange juice, toast, coffee, and ham and eggs. (*Ham and eggs* is considered to be one unit.)

10. The comma is used to separate coordinate adjectives which modify the same noun. Adjectives are coordinate adjectives which modify the same noun. Adjectives are coordinate if the word *and* can be used between them.

The efficient, business-like secretary received an advance in pay. (Comma—the efficient *and* business-like secretary. Both adjectives modify *secretary.*)

The five silver spoons were very expensive. (No comma—you would not say *five and silver spoons.*)

11. The comma is used in a compound sentence to separate independent clauses joined by one of the coordinate conjunctions *and, but, for, or, nor,* and *while* when it means the same as *but.* See Chapter Seventeen for a detailed discussion of compound sentences.)

I dictated the letter as you ordered, but she did not transcribe it correctly.

Minneapolis is a large industrial center, and it has many cultural
attractions.

(a) If the clauses of a compound sentence are very short and
closely connected, the comma may be omitted.

He looked but he did not see her.

(b) Do not use a comma between two independent clauses
unless a coordinate conjunction is used. The use of a comma
without a coordinate conjunction between two independent
clauses is called the *comma fault*. The following sentence illustrates the comma fault:

The men in the shipping department will not follow instructions, they repeatedly make serious errors. (Incorrect—comma
should not be used without a coordinate conjunction.)

Note 1: The comma fault may be eliminated by punctuating
the sentence in one of the three following ways:

(a) Use a coordinate conjunction after the comma:

The men in the shipping department will not follow instructions, and they repeatedly make serious errors. (correct)

(b) Use a semicolon between the two independent clauses:

The men in the shipping department will not follow instructions; they repeatedly make serious errors. (correct—see Rule
1 under semicolons.)

(c) Punctuate the two independent clauses as two simple sentences:

The men in the shipping department will not follow instructions. They repeatedly make serious errors. (correct)

Note 2: When the independent clauses of a compound sentence
are very long or have *internal punctuation*, a semicolon is
generally used before the coordinate conjunction. Internal

punctuation means that there are commas within one or both of the independent clauses.

Copyboy, take this folder to Alan Toms, the fellow in brown over there; and be sure to come back.

Quietly efficient, Joan continued in her position; but she never got the raise.

Both of these sentences have one or more commas in the first independent clause. Since the first clause has internal punctuation, a semicolon is used between the two independent clauses even though a coordinate conjunction is used. (See Rule 3 under semicolons.)

12. The comma is used to set off words or phrases expressing contrast.

I asked you to file the contract, not destroy it.

You may be excused from the conference this time, but never again.

Children should be seen, not heard.

13. The comma is used to set off a definite place, month, or year.

Cleveland, Ohio	July 12, 1986
Cook County, Illinois	in December, 1985

Or, in sentence form, the comma is used in the following manner:

The president was born April 8, 1872, at 1224 Elm Street, Cleveland, Ohio.

14. The comma is used to set off a direct quotation.

The director asked, "How many of you are in favor of this change in policy?"

15. The comma is used as a substitute for an exclamation point after a mild interjection.

Well, I'm glad that's over.
My, it's really raining.

16. The comma is used after inverted names.

Thackeray, William M.
Whittier, John Greenleaf

17. The comma is used to indicate the omission of a word.

Fishing forms a quiet man; hunting, an eager man; racing, a greedy man.

18. The comma is used to set off a proper name when followed by an academic degree or honorary title. the comma is used to separate two or more degrees or titles.

Philip F. Adams, A.B., M.A., Ph.D., lecturer in English.

19. The comma is used to point off the thousands in figures of four digits or more.

1,117   20,718   1,817,000

Note: Do not use the comma in street addresses, page and policy numbers, or in years.

the year 1985   Policy No. 903451
page 2348   1117 Pensacola Ave.

20. The comma is used to separate two sets of figures or two identical words.

John told you, you should apply immediately.
Send me 10, No. 1234 and 7, No. 138.
Since 1986, 12,000 new machines have been sold.

21. The comma is used to separate a declarative clause and an interrogative clause which immediately follows.

The plane will arrive on time, will it not?
Jack is to get a promotion, isn't he?

22. The comma is used to separate a phrase from the rest of the sentence when the phrase is inverted or out of its natural order.

Like you, I think the policy is a worthwhile one.
For me, it will mean extra work and less pay.
In spite of his promise, he was late to work again.

USE OF THE SEMICOLON

The semicolon (;) is used to show a stronger separation between the parts of a sentence than does a comma. In practical writing, however, avoid using the semicolon because it is generally too stiff and formal. If you use a great many semicolons, the chances are that you are either using them incorrectly, or you are writing sentences which are too long. Semicolons produce rather involved sentence patterns. Use them sparingly.

1. The semicolon is used to separate independent coordinate clauses closely connected in meaning when no coordinate conjunction is used.

The sales staff meets every other Tuesday; the production staff meets only once a month.

He would not approve the art layout as presented; he suggested several drastic changes.

Note: An example of this rule, as used to avoid the comma fault, was given in Rule 11 under commas.

2. The semicolon is used between coordinate clauses of a compound sentence when they are joined by transitional words and phrases. The following is a list of commonly used transitional words and phrases:

accordingly	indeed	as a result
afterwards	likewise	at last

again	meanwhile	at the same time
anyhow	moreover	for example
besides	namely	for instance
consequently	nevertheless	for this reason
doubtless	next	in any case
eventually	otherwise	in fact
evidently	perhaps	in like manner
finally	possibly	in short
furthermore	still	on the contrary
hence	then	on the other hand
however	therefore	that is
yet	thus	in addition

For a further discussion of transitional words, see chapter 17.

Note: You have already learned that transitional words are usually set off by commas. When you use a semicolon in place of a comma before the transitional word, you usually put a comma after the transitional word. However, when the transitional word retains its adverbial force and is not regarded as an independent element, it is seldom set off with a comma.

The members of the board of directors approved the change in distribution; consequently, you should appeal to them.

The weather was cold and icy; therefore we didn't go.

3. The semicolon is used before a coordinate conjunction (*and, but, for, or, nor*) between two independent clauses when either one or both have internal punctuation.

The president, a well-read man, predicted a cost of living increase for the first of the year; but his prediction, which spread throughout the plant, proved to be wrong.

The staff housekeeper ordered carpets, divans, lamps, tables, and chairs; but her order was incorrectly filled.

4. The semicolon is used before such words as *for example*, *for instance*, *that is*, and *namely* that introduce an example, enumeration, or a list in a sentence. A comma is placed after such words.

These special artist's pencils are available in three colors; namely, red, green, and blue.

Many of our policies will be changed this year; for example, salesmen will be paid a commission instead of a salary.

5. The semicolon is used in lists where a comma is insufficient to separate the members clearly.

Guests at the convention were Mr. Leonard Key, the past president of the corporation; Mrs. F. K. Small, the wife of the founder; and Mr. Paul Wells, the speaker of the evening.

USE OF THE COLON

The colon (:) indicates the strongest possible break within a sentence.

1. The colon is used before a list of items or details.

Please send out the following items: No. 378, No. 315, No. 519, and No. 570.

His actions were as follows: He went to the drugstore, purchased a hypodermic needle, got into his car, and drove away.

Note 1: Capitalize the first letter of each item in a list when the list is in column form.

You should know how to use the following office machines:

1. Typewriter
2. Duplicator
3. Copy Machine
4. Calculator

237

Note 2: Do not capitalize the first letter of each item in a list when the items are included in a sentence.

You should know how to use the following office machines: typewriter, duplicator, copy machine, and calculator.

2. The colon is used before an appositive phrase or clause.

Our company has always had this motto: The customer is always right.

These are your duties: Sort the mail, open all that is not personal, throw away the envelopes, and bring the letters to me.

Note: Capitalize the first letter of the word which follows the colon when that word introduces a complete sentence, as in the above examples.

3. The colon is used after the salutation of a business letter.

Dear Mr. Roe: Gentlemen: My Dear Madam:

Note: Never use a semicolon after a salutation. A comma may be used after the salutation of a friendly or informal letter.

Dear Jane,   Dear Father,   Dear Jones,

4. The colon is used to divide the parts of references, titles, formulas, and numerals.

The time was 9:15 p.m.
He assigned Chapter XII: Section 19.

USE OF PARENTHESES

1. Parentheses () are used to set off words, phrases, clauses, or sentences which are used by way of explanation, translation, or comment, but which are independent constructions:

Hilda (my sister's roommate at college) is coming to visit us.
The motto read as follows: *"De gustibus non disputandum est."* (In matters of taste there is no dispute.)

2. Parentheses are used to enclose a number, letter, or symbol when used as an appositive.

She ordered twelve (12) night stands for the hotel.
The bookkeeper ornamented his letterhead with the percent symbol (%).

Note 1: When using parentheses with other punctuation marks, punctuate the main part of the sentence as if the parenthetical portion was not there. A punctuation mark comes after the second parenthesis if the punctuation mark applies to the whole sentence and not just to the parenthetical portion.

He analyzed and presented standards of evaluation (business and technical), but his conditions proved nothing.

Note 2: Place the punctuation mark inside the second parenthesis if the punctuation mark applies only to material within the parenthetical portion.

A simplified fire-fighting plan will help you. (See the back cover of this brochure.)

USE OF THE DASH

The dash (—) is used to indicate an abrupt change of ideas, but should be used sparingly. Excessive use of the dash usually indicates that the writer does not know what punctuation mark to use.

There are times you may want to use the dash for visual effect or emphasis. A glance at advertisements in a newspaper shows that copy writers make frequent use of the dash. However, in business writing, such as letters, reports, minutes, and in social correspondence, use the dash with caution.

1. The dash may be used to indicate a sudden change of thought in a sentence.

I was certain that the manager—indeed, all of the office force—wanted John to receive the promotion.

2. The dash may be used to indicate a summarizing thought or an afterthought added to the end of the sentence.

I shall make out an estimate, draw up a contract, send out a man to interpret it for you—give you every help I can.

3. The dash may be used to set off a word or phrase repeated for emphasis.

We invited them for one meeting—one meeting only—not for the entire convention!

4. The dash may be used between numbers or dates to indicate *to* and *and*.

His chapter covered from 1860—1868.
My appointment was scheduled from 12:15—1:15.

Note on the punctuation of parenthetical matter: Close study of the rules on commas, parentheses, and dashes will show you that any one of the three punctuation marks may be used to set off parenthetical words, phrases, or clauses. When should you use the commas, dash, or parentheses? No strict rule can be stated. In general, follow this practice: In punctuating parenthetical matter, use dashes mainly for visual effect; use commas if the material is short; and use parentheses if the material is long.

USE OF BRACKETS

1. Brackets [ ] are used to enclose material added by someone other than the writer; for example, editorial additions or comments.

The investigation [from June 1, 1985 to April 8, 1986] caused considerable speculation.

The poet [Robert Browning] did not approve of the excessive adulation during the meeting.

2. Brackets are used to enclose parenthetical matter within parenthetical matter.

Your order (including items No. 391, No. 394, and No. 286 [No. 288 was out of stock]) was filled last week.

Note: Brackets are rarely used in business and social writing. Generally they are found only in printed material of a scholarly or technical nature.

USE OF THE QUESTION MARK

1. The question mark (**?**) is used after all interrogative sentences that ask direct questions.

Where are the current files?
Are you going to the next meeting of the club?

Note: After requests, use a period instead of a question mark. (See Rule 2 under periods.)

2. The question mark may be used after each separate part of a sentence containing more than one question.

Can we be sure of his willingness? his capability? his honesty?

Note: If the question is not complete until the end of the sentence, place a question mark at the end only.

Will delivery be made today, tomorrow, or Friday?

3. The question mark is used in several ways when only part of the sentence is a question. In such sentences the question is generally introduced by a comma or colon; a semicolon or dash may also be used.

May I ask, what is his purpose?
This is our problem: What should be done to prevent further damage?
Our questions are, what date will you arrive? where will you stay? and, do you desire us to furnish transportation?

USE OF THE EXCLAMATION MARK

1. The exclamation mark (!) is used after all exclamatory sentences—sentences that express surprise, emotion, or deep feeling.

Look out for that train!
Headlines read, ''Peace Treaty Signed!''
Your answer was hard to believe!

2. The exclamation mark is used after an interjection or a word used as an interjection. At times, the sentence following the interjection may be exclamatory.

Hurry! The train will pull out in three minutes!
Oh! I haven't heard that before.

3. The exclamation mark is used after statements which are commands or which imply need for immediate action.

Return the card today! Don't delay!
Hurry! Send your order now!

4. The exclamation point is used after an interrogative sentence that is exclamatory in form or intended to be exclamatory.

Oh, how could he say that!
But can he be trusted!

5. The exclamation point is sometimes used to add emphasis.

Realize what this means!
This offer absolutely expires April 6!

USE OF QUOTATION MARKS

1. Quotation marks ('' '') are used to enclose a direct quotation. Each part of an interrupted quotation begins and ends with quotation marks.

The inspector said, ''Well, your case is not hopeless.''
''Where,'' he asked, ''are you going to keep it?''

"What will we do?" he asked. "Where can we raise the
money?"

Note: Capitalize the first word of a direct quotation. Do not
capitalize the first word in the second part of an interrupted
quotation unless the second part begins a new sentence. Do
not use quotation marks or capital letters in an indirect quotation.

The inspector said that your case is not hopeless. (Many indirect
quotations are introduced by the word *that*.)
He asked where we would keep it.

   2. Quotation marks are used to enclose the titles of magazine
articles, chapters of books, names of songs, titles of poems,
and other titles.

The New Yorker includes a section entitled "The Talk of the
Town."
She asked Ellen to sing "Because" at her wedding.
"Rabbi Ben Ezra" is one of my favorite poems.
Note: In typing or writing, underline the titles of books, mag-
azines, operas, and any other works of art long enough to
appear in book form. Underlining signifies italics for printing.
The words, "The New Yorker" in the first sentence above are
printed in italic type.

The anthology, <u>Toward Liberal Education,</u> includes A. E.
Housman's "Introductory Lecture" and S. I. Hayakawa's
"Poetry and Advertising."

The soprano sang "If Madam Should Call You" from Mozart's
<u>Marriage of Figaro.</u>

   3. Quotation marks are used to set off words, phrases, or
sentences referred to within a sentence.

The word "proceed" is frequently mispronounced.

The phrase "on the other hand" is sometimes used as a transitional phrase.

The sentence "Now is the time for all good men to come to the aid of their party" is an excellent typing exercise.

4. Quotation marks are used to set off slang words or expressions.

She said that the office party was held at a "swank" hotel.

5. If several paragraphs are quoted, use quotation marks at the beginning of each paragraph but at the end of the last paragraph only. Long quotations are usually introduced by a colon instead of a comma. Quotations of three or more lines are usually indented and set apart from the body of the text.

USE OF QUOTATION MARKS WITH OTHER PUNCTUATION

(a) The period and comma are always placed before ending quotation marks.

He said, "They are not here."
"They are not here," he said.

(b) The question mark and exclamation point are placed before quotation marks when they refer only to the quoted material.

She asked, "When are you going to be promoted?"

(c) The question mark and exclamation point follow ending quotation marks when they refer to the entire sentence.

Did she say, "You are to be promoted next month"?

(d) The semicolon and colon follow ending quotation marks unless they are part of the quoted matter.

She said, "You are to be promoted next month"; consequently, I expected to be promoted.

USE OF SINGLE QUOTATION MARKS

1. Single quotation marks are used to set off a quotation within a quotation.

"Jane," I asked, "did you tell me how to spell the word 'pathologically'?"

The irate mother said, "You must get all of this 'junk' out of the living room at once."

Note: Other punctuation marks are used with single quotation marks in the same way as with double quotation marks.

USE OF THE APOSTROPHE

1. The apostrophe (') is used in nouns to show possession.

Note: Keep in mind that the sign of the possessive case is always added to a word. It is not something that is inserted within a word.

(a) If the singular form of the noun does not end in **s** or an **s** sound, add the apostrophe and **s** (**'s**).

Singular	Singular Possessive
boy	boy's
girl	girl's
lady	lady's

(b) If the singular ends in **s** or an **s** sound, add the apostrophe (') or the apostrophe and **s** (**'s**) if the additional **s** sound is desired.

Singular	Singular Possessive
boss	boss' or boss's
dress	dress' or dress's
box	box' or box's

(c) If the plural form of the noun does not end in **s**, add the apostrophe and **s** (**s'**)

Plural	Plural Possessive
men	men's
children	children's
mice	mice's
teeth	teeth's
geese	geese's

(d) If the plural form of the noun ends in **s,** add the apostrophe (**'**)

Plural	Plural Possessive
boys	boys'
girls	girls'
ladies	ladies'

(e) The possessives of proper nouns are formed in the same way as the possessives of common nouns. If the singular form of the name does not end in **s**, add the apostrophe and **s**. If the singular ends in **s** or an **s** sound, add the apostrophe (**'**) or the apostrophe and **s** (**'s**). The plural possessive is always formed by adding the apostrophe to the plural form.

Proper Noun	Singular Possess- ive	Plural	Plural Possess- ive
John	John's	Johns	Johns'
Phyllis	Phyllis' or Phyllis's	Phyllises	Phyllises'
Jane	Jane's	Janes	Janes'

(f) Certain expressions relating to *time, distance,* and *value* are also written with an apostrophe.

the day's task	five cents's worth
a year's time	six miles' distance
a minute's notice	three weeks' vacation

(g) The singular possessive and the plural possessive of compound nouns are formed by adding the apostrophe to the end of the compound word.

Singular

brother-in-law's
father-in-law's

Plural

brothers-in-law's
fathers-in-law's

(h) Joint ownership is shown by making the last word in the series possessive. Individual ownership is shown by making both parts possessive.

Alice and Jack's apartment. (joint ownership)
Alice's and Jack's apartments. (individual ownership)

2. The apostrophe is used in indefinite pronouns to show possession. The possessive case of indefinite pronouns is formed in the same way as the possessive case of nouns.

everybody's duty
one's coat

others' positions
someone's hat

3. The apostrophe is used with **s** to form the plural of numbers, letters, signs, and symbols.

Your "r's" look like "n's."
He used twelve "r's" to decorate his paper.

4. The apostrophe is used to indicate the omission of a word, letters, or numerals.

don't	let's	o'clock
hadn't	it's	she's
isn't	'tis	wouldn't

The accident happened in '86.